The Database Experts'
Guide to
SQL

The Database Experts'
Guide to
SQL

Frank Lusardi

Intertext Publications/Multiscience Press, Inc.
McGraw-Hill, Inc. New York, NY

Library of Congress Catalog Card Number 87–83099

10 9 8 7 6 5 4 3 2 1

ISBN 0–07–039006–1 (Hardcover)
ISBN 0–07–039002–9 (Paperback)

SQL is a trademark of International Business Machines, Inc.
DB2 is a trademark of International Business Machines, Inc.

Intertext Publications/Multiscience Press, Inc.
McGraw-Hill Book Company
1221 Avenue of the Americas
New York, NY 10020

Contents

Take things as they come.

INSERT INTO CHARACTER VALUES
('PATIENCE', 'CURIOSITY');

FIGURES

Preface

For a web begun, God sends thread.

UPDATE PROJECT
SET STARTDATE = 'TODAY';

Structured Query Language, having recently been declared an American standard by the American National Standards Institute (ANSI), is fast becoming the *lingua franca* of the computer database world. Mainframe and minicomputer relational database products have been released in versions which run on microcomputers, and they have, of course, brought SQL with them. Microcomputer database products which never were and never will be relational are providing SQL as a means of downloading mainframe data. It is to be hoped that it will not prove long before all SQL links will be made two-way streets, allowing databases of all architectures, running on computers of all architectures, to query one another and to exchange data.

This book will address itself to all those who do or will use SQL to "get some work done." It is intended for the user who is "interactive" with SQL day-to-day and for the programmer who needs to "reach out and touch" a database. Those who are just getting started with databases will not find it unfriendly.

The book is practical-minded; more "tips and techniques" than theory. It will discuss what can be done with SQL (or at least what the author has done with it) and how you may do these things. The emphasis has been placed not on theory, but on design; we will not create tables without thinking what other tables have been or will be created and what structures we might use to link them.

The book will discuss all that is in the ANSI standard and much that is not. It will range beyond SQL proper, to applications into which SQL is embedded, such as report writers, interactive forms, and programs. In doing so it will leave behind specific implementations of these applications— you may find that your report writer gets rather upset if you give it some syntax straight out of this book. But the *techniques* will hold; you will easily translate the author's tricks into your own.

Many SQL statements have been included in the text of the book. Figures within each chapter include SQL statements along with their results. All SQL statements and their results may be compared with the underlying tables and their data, which are printed in Appendix A.

Throughout the book, *Technotes* discuss particular points in added depth and *DesignNotes* discuss how particulars might affect the overall design of a database system.

To many people, computer languages seem as dry as dust. But this dust has a way of living: It is born, grows and changes, has successes and failures, is accepted or discarded and forgotten. A language touches lives, molds careers, and can create whole industries. This book attempts, in Appendix D, to give the reader a glimpse of SQL alive in the "real world," pleasing some and exasperating others.

A quick reference to SQL syntax has been included in Appendix F.

Acknowledgments

I would like to thank my publisher, Alan Rose, for his encouragement and enthusiasm. I would like to thank a former colleague, Esther Sukhra, who paid no heed to SQL's limitations and made it do what needed doing. This book—the text, tables, headers, front and back matter—was typeset by the author using Donald Knuth's program TEX.

New York City, 1988   Frank Lusardi

1. The Language and Its Subject

Hearts that are kind,
and tongues that are not,
these are the best company.

SELECT PERSON FROM PEOPLE
WHERE HEART = 'KIND' AND
MIND = 'SKEPTICAL';

1.1   This Language Among Others

Structured Query Language, or SQL—pronounced "sequel"—is a language much like any other; it uses words and symbols to construct sentences which express ideas. Like other languages the number of sentences which it may form and, therefore, the number of ideas which it may express, is without bound. Like the mathematical languages, SQL is strictly defined and extremely limited in its verbs; the separate types of actions which it may take comprise only a handful. Like the natural languages, SQL is entirely unlimited in its nouns; it may act upon revenues and ravens, gross receipts and galaxies.

Although it does not limit the *matter* which may be stored, SQL strictly confines the *manner* in which its subjects may be held. It insists that it will accept information only if it has been divided into carefully structured pieces, and only if the structure of each piece agrees exactly with certain carefully defined structure *types*. Information which has been clipped and categorized in this manner is called DATA and a collection of such information, an expanse of data, whether large or small, is called a DATABASE.

1

TABLE							
field	field		field	field	field	field	field
field	field	C	field	field	field	field	field
Jennifer	Mallory	O	Lawyer	11/11/1965	44 W. 12th	New York	10016
field	field	L	field	field	field	field	field
←		U	— ROW, or Record				→
field	field	M	field	field	field	field	field
field	field	N	field	field	field	field	field
field	field		field	field	field	field	field

Figure 1.1   The parts of a table.

The verbs of the language, very limited in number, all concern the creation, maintenance, and, most frequently, the probing of a database. It is this last function, the asking for or selecting of particular bits of data from a large collection, which defines SQL as a QUERY LANGUAGE.

The strictures placed upon the language pertain solely to its structure and to the arrangement of the information which it stores and retrieves. Neither SQL nor its data definitions impose any constraint upon what matters might be cataloged for viewing, or how these subjects might be gathered together to form new subjects.

Like any other language, SQL will be for you what you make of it: subtle or clumsy; flowing or hesitant; a welcome tool or a difficult imposition.

1.2   The Relational Architecture

Just as there are carefully categorized types of data, there are types of databases. The types correspond to the internal structure, or *architecture* of the database. The elements of the architecture, the girders and gables, determine how the structure may be approached and entered. The database gives birth to the database language; the elements of the database architecture determine how the contents of the database may be addressed. The database architecture which gave birth to SQL is called RELATIONAL.

The basic building block of the relational architecture is a structure called a TABLE. A database, even a very large one, may contain only one table, or it may contain many tables, but there can be no database if there are no tables. The table structure is in turn composed of smaller structures, the ROW and COLUMN. A table could consist of only one row and a number of columns; or of one column and a number of rows; or even of only one column and one row; but there can be no table if there are no rows and no columns. If you think of a database table as a rectangular object—and you *should* view it as such—then the rows would run horizontally across the table and the columns would run vertically up and down. If this paragraph were a table, then each line of text would be a row and, well, we would be hard pressed to find columns—perhaps the last letter of each line, all neatly aligned, might constitute a column; or we could say that our makeshift table had but one column, a column which held a full line of text.

> *TechNote:* Not all "relational" databases are indeed relational in their inner structure. The popularity of SQL and the relational model has prompted the makers of many non-relational database products to provide SQL as a means of access, or "front-end" to their products. There is nothing dishonest or necessarily deficient in this, but doing it well is difficult—since SQL is not "natural" to the database, each SQL statement must first be translated into whatever language the product normally accepts, thereby adding one more step to the fetch operation, or any other operation. It is as if the *Committee for Granting Requests* one day decreed that, as an added service to the populace, it would accept requests and issue decisions in Spanish, as well as in its native English. You could be certain that, no matter how slowly or quickly the Committee normally processed a request, it would require *more* time for one submitted in Spanish, because there would be a translation procedure added to the already existing procedures.

Rows Are Records, Columns Are Fields

As with all useful and used constructs, the relational database model carries with it its baggage of terms and their synonyms: A row in a table is also known as a RECORD, and any given piece of a row which fits into a column is called a FIELD. A row, or record, will consist of fields, marching side by side across the table. A column will consist of fields stacked one upon another, running down the table from top to bottom.

If we had a table which contained only one record, and which record contained but one field, we would have the most minimal of tables, for the field is the atom of the relational model and cannot be subdivided. It is this object, the field, which must conform in its structure to one of the basic data types—a character, an integer, a decimal number, etc.

1.3   The Four Subdivisions

SQL verbs may be conveniently grouped into four categories, depending upon the type of action which they perform. The functions performed in these four categories are common to all databases, of whatever architecture. The functions are: the creation and deletion of structures within the database; the filling of these structures with data, and the removal of data from structures; the inquiries performed upon the data, so as to discover

THE SQL SUBDIVISIONS	
DIVISION	VERBS
Queries	Select
Data Manipulation Language (DML)	Insert Update Delete
Data Definition Language (DDL)	Create Drop
Data Control Language (DCL)	Grant

Figure 1.2   The four subdivisions.

what bits and pieces are there, and how they are related; and the "security" functions, which allow certain users to see or not see certain bits of data.

Queries

In SQL the verb is SELECT. These are the statements which probe the database and retrieve information. They may cause related information to be grouped or disparate information to be linked. In normal usage, the SELECT statements are far and away the most often called upon parts of the language. An example would be:

    SELECT FNAME, LNAME, ADDRESS FROM PERSONNEL
    WHERE FNAME = 'Barbara';

It is, of course, because of its frequent use in exercising queries that SQL is called a "query language."

Data Manipulation Language (DML)

The verbs are INSERT, UPDATE, and DELETE. These are the statements which add records to a table, alter the data within those records, and remove records from a table. An example would be:

    DELETE FROM PERSONNEL WHERE FNAME = 'Barbara';

These verbs are the ones that will be used most often by those unsung heroes and heroines of all database installations, the "data entry" staff—it is often forgotten that not one of the millions of bits of information in a typical database gets into the database without someone putting it there.

Data Definition Language (DDL)

The verbs are CREATE and DROP. These statements create or delete database tables. An example would be:

DROP TABLE PERSONNEL;

Data Control Language (DCL)

The verb is GRANT. These are the security statements, granting or revoking the privileges needed to view tables within the database. These statements will be used by the DATABASE ADMINISTRATOR to enforce decisions concerning who may or may not use certain database tables. An example would be:

GRANT SELECT ON PERSONNEL TO JONES;

1.4   Tables Here, Tables There

You are surrounded by tables, tables of information, tables in the *relational* sense of the word. You use their rows and columns, records and fields every day. You associate one field with another because they appear in the same record, and then again you associate field to field because they stand in the same column.

With a new language we may create familiar things in unfamiliar ways—in SQL we may create the most common of things in this way:

```
CREATE TABLE MONTH
(SUN NUMBER(2), MON NUMBER(2), TUE NUMBER(2),
WED NUMBER(2), THU NUMBER(2), FRI NUMBER(2),
SAT NUMBER(2), SUN NUMBER (2));
```

But our common thing would be empty, without content. We may fill it in this way:

INSERT INTO MONTH VALUES(1,2,3,4,5,6,7);

INSERT INTO MONTH VALUES(8,9,10,11,12,13,14);

INSERT INTO MONTH VALUES(15,16,17,18,19,20,21);

INSERT INTO MONTH VALUES(22,23,24,25,26,27,28);

INSERT INTO MONTH VALUES(29,30,31,NULL,NULL,NULL,NULL);

And were we to request a glimpse at our creation in this manner:

SELECT * FROM MONTH;

we would be shown the following:

SUN	MON	TUE	WED	THU	FRI	SAT
1	2	3	4	5	6	7
8	9	10	11	12	13	14
15	16	17	18	19	20	21
22	23	24	25	26	27	28
29	30	31				

Each number in our table is a field. A record, or row, would be any set of fields which comprise one week. A column would be all of those numbers which fall under one particular day.

And we might create a very familiar, very large, white table by executing statements such as the following:

INSERT INTO WPAGE VALUES
('Crandwell', 'Margaret', 'A', '222 E 11', '645-5575');

1.5   The Atoms of the Architecture

Relational database tables may be broken down into rows and columns. A row may contain a number of fields, and a column may consist of a number of fields. But the field, the unit of which all these structures are made, cannot be subdivided. The field is the basic building block of the database, the atom. The fact that fields may not be subdivided, that they are the smallest unit of the architecture, does not necessarily mean that each individual field is small—a field can be quite substantial; a text field might be large enough to hold an entire sentence, or paragraph.

> *TechNote:* Fields may be subdivided *after* they have been extracted from the database. An SQL OPERATOR may be used, for instance, to extract just the month value from a date field, but before this operation may be performed, the entire date field must be extracted from the database, extracted as a *unit*.

1.6   The Types of Data

Just as a chemical element is defined by the structure of the atoms which comprise it, relational database fields can be devided into types which are defined by their *structure*. Whenever you create a field within a table you will be required to specify the structure of the field by naming its *type*. In selecting the field type you will be restricted to the types which are available in the particular database product which you are using. The field types available in a particular product will vary, but will always consist of a subset or superset of the following: numeric fields, both integer and decimal; character fields; time and date fields.

SQL FIELD TYPES	
TYPE	EXAMPLES
Integer	12
	865400
	0
	1985
Decimal	12.1
	865.412
	0
	1985
Character	A
	Baseball
	Mary Lee
	1985
Date	9/9/75
	12-25-1985

Figure 1.3   The field types.

The Integer

An integer field is numeric and is signed, meaning that it may contain either a positive or a negative number. It may not contain a fractional part (no decimal point is allowed). The allowed characters are therefore the numbers 0-9 and the '+' and '−' signs.

The Decimal

A decimal field is numeric and is signed and may contain a fractional part. The allowed characters are the numbers 0-9, the decimal point, '.', and the '+' and '-' signs.

TechNote: Some relational database implementations allow for the creation of both integer and decimal fields under one field type called *number*, or something similar. In this case you must very specifically, within the definition, disallow decimal numbers, if you want a field to accept only integers. This book will use the number field convention. The means for restricting such fields to integer values or values with a specific number of decimal places will be discussed in the chapter on creating tables. Normally, you will be allowed to specify a length for each portion of the number, and a non decimal number would be defined as having a decimal portion of zero length.

The Character

In computer applications, groups of letters or numbers, or both, are often referred to as "strings." A string is a collection of characters, usually including any "displayable" character. The displayable characters are usually all of those which you find on your computer keyboard. The word "character" is a string. This sentence is a string. The numerals and all punctuation marks are displayable characters. "12@&*56-+)=" is a string. When defining a field which will contain characters you will usually be required to specify a *length*, i.e. the maximum number of characters which the field may contain. A string of length one may contain only a single character. You cannot define a character field as having a length of zero, but zero-length strings do exist. A string containing no characters is called a "null string" and is often denoted with side-by-side quotation marks; "".

Time and Date

Our exploration of possible field structures must now step into some controversy. Although fields designed specifically to hold date and time information are tremendously useful (so much so that many consider them indispensable—as you will once you have used them), there are relational database products, even old and well-established ones, which do *not* include such fields in their repertoire. The ANSI standard does not include such fields. If such fields exist in the database implementation which you are using, then their meaning is straightforward—a date field will accept a date, a properly formatted date, and will accept nothing else; a time field will accept only a properly formatted time. "Properly formatted" means that the numbers denoting the month will be separated from the numbers denoting the day by a certain character (a "delimiter") acceptable to the database, and so on for numbers denoting year, hour, minute, second. One implementation may accept a slash ('/') as a date delimiter and another may accept a hyphen ('-'), and yet another may allow you to use either. One or both of the following should be accceptable to your particular implementation: 12-25-85, 12/25/1985. A date without delimiters, such as 122485, will most likely be unacceptable in any date field.

The Null

The null is not a field *type*, but it is a curious animal whose domain includes all of the field types, and you should come to know its ways as early on as possible. A null may inhabit any field type, if you allow it; or you may banish it when you define the field. We will discuss including and excluding nulls when we discuss table creation. We will discuss using nulls when we discuss queries. Here we will define it—it is nothing. A null field is one which has nothing in it. Any field of any type *may* be null. All nulls are alike. A null date field is exactly the same as a null decimal field. A zero is *not* a null. A numeric field which contains a zero is fully occupied. A space is *not* a null. A character field which contains nothing but a single space is fully occupied. A field of any type that is not occupied, which contains nothing, is a null field.

> *TechNote:* How does a database store something which is not there? How do you place into a field something which means that nothing has been placed there? Well, you don't, you can't. Fields which may accept a null value will have attached to them, within the database, a second, hidden field, a "flag" field. When the field is null, the database will "set" the flag; when the field is occupied, the flag will be "cleared." This is of consequence in terms of the space needed within a database to store a given field. If a field is to be allowed to accept null values, then the database must allocate space for the flag field in addition to space for the field itself. The additional space required is usually very small in comparison to the space required for the field itself.

1.7   The ANSI Standard

The American National Standards Institute, located in New York City, publishes technical specifications for a wide range of computer devices and languages. The standards are developed by committees whose members usually represent associations and corporations which are active in using or manufacturing the specified devices and languages. ANSI standards are entirely voluntary; manufacturers are free to use or disregard them as they wish. The ANSI Database Committee, known as X3H2, approved the SQL standard in October 1986. The organizations represented in developing the SQL standard included: Association for Computing Machinery; AT&T; Digital Equipment Corp.; Eastman Kodak; General Electric; Hewlett Packard; IBM; Wang; Xerox.

1.8   What's It All About?

Why learn SQL? Perhaps you have to. Perhaps your boss has hinted that you will learn SQL or your position will be filled by someone who has. Perhaps you have just spent $600 on a database package which is to bring organization to your life and you have discovered that it only speaks SQL. Perhaps you are a programmer who has been quite content with COBOL for all these years and are suddenly faced with having to get information from and put information into a relational database. Perhaps you are just embarrassed—your colleague knows SQL and it is wearisome to have to always ask. Perhaps you want to learn how *not* to design a query language (SQL has many shortcomings).

Whatever your motivation, you may enliven the learning by pursuing in your mind not only the *how* of SQL but the *why*. Does knowledge lend itself to be structured as tables? Does all knowledge? What facts refuse to be ordered in rows and columns, and why? Can all questioning be reduced to a single word, *select*? If it cannot be then what do we lose when we accept SQL? Can we structure our data, arrange the tables so as to empower our queries with more versatility, more subtlety?

2. The Getting of Information

The shortest answer is doing.

SELECT PLANS FROM POSSIBILITIES
WHERE PROBABILITY > 90;

2.1   The Select Statement

How old is Jennifer Mallory? How much did the Advertising Department spend last year? How far is Mars from the Sun? How, what, where, when, who? All of the English interrogatives, all of the words for the requesting, the demanding, the cajoling, the wheedling of answers come down to one word in SQL—SELECT.

If you know that one word, SELECT, and the name of a table, then you need only the word *from*, an asterisk (*), and a semicolon (;) in order to extract from that table all the information which it contains. The syntax of the basic SELECT statement is as follows (the reader should consult the tables listed in Appendix A in conjunction with all examples used in this book):

SELECT * FROM PEOPLE;

SELECT * FROM MOONS;

The word SELECT is the verb, the command, the query. The asterisk is a shorthand way of saying "all columns." The statement "select *" (pronounced "select star"—an asterisk is often referred to as a "star") is a request to see every column in the table. The word *from* merely lets your computer know that the next word will be the name of a table in the database. If you follow the word *from* with anything but the name of a table, your computer will present you with an error message. The semicolon is used in SQL to terminate a statement. It is the equivalent of the period used to end an English sentence. We will soon see that, just as an English sentence may continue for more than a single line, so may a SQL statement. There must be some special mark which tells the computer that it has reached the end of a statement, that it now has all of the statement, and that it may begin to process that statement. In SQL that special mark is a semicolon.

> *TechNote:* The ANSI standard declares that there are to be some matters which will *not* be standardized. The "end-of-line indicator" is one of these. The character used to mark the end of a SQL statement is left to be defined by the SQL implementor. The ANSI standard is derived largely from the SQL implementation used by IBM in its relational database DB2. DB2 uses the semicolon as the end-of-line indicator. It is a fairly safe bet that anyone implementing SQL will choose the semicolon as end-of-line indicator.

Instead of using an asterisk to request all fields we can write out the list of all fields, separating the field names with commas:

SELECT ID, FNAME, LNAME, PROF,
BIRTH, CITY, STATE FROM PEOPLE;

SELECT PLANET, NAME, DISTANCE,
DIAMETER FROM MOONS;

These commands would deliver up to us exactly what the previous ones did: the same data in the same arrangement. And with this command we come to the end of what may be done with an asterisk. If you wish to be shown all of the fields from a table in the order in which they were created when the table was created, then you can use the asterisk. In you wish to see anything other than that, then the asterisk will be of no use to you. The asterisk is handy when you are at a computer terminal and "interactive" with SQL, when you need to splash a lot of data on the screen, or when you are casting about for something which you know you put *somewhere* in the database. But you will find that you usually want to see less than everything.

> *TechNote:* We will see later on that the asterisk can be downright dangerous when used in a report writer or in a SQL statement embedded within a programming language. The problem is that asking for "everything" from a table tomorrow may result in greater or fewer fields than asking today. Tables can be changed. This problem illustrates,

SELECT TUE, WED, THU FROM MONTH;

TUE	WED	THU
3	4	5
10	11	12
17	18	19
24	25	26
31		

Figure 2.1   The result of a select statement is a new table.

---

in general, the difference between "interactive" and "embedded" uses of SQL. Interaction is by definition subject to daily change. Reports and programs are intended to produce over time the *same* results— perhaps with more or less data, but not with *different* data.

If you wish to view only certain fields, then list only those fields in your query:

SELECT NAME, DISTANCE FROM S_SYSTEM;

SELECT FNAME, LNAME, PROF FROM PEOPLE;

If you wish to view fields in some other order, list the fields in that order:

SELECT BIRTH, LNAME, FNAME FROM PEOPLE;

SELECT LNAME, FNAME, BIRTH, STATE FROM PEOPLE;

Given the name of a table and the names of its fields you may use the above simple commands to retrieve the data contained within all of the fields or within any subset of fields, in whatever order you wish. What you *cannot* do with the above commands is limit the number of *records* that you will be shown. If our table contained records for 10,000 people and you selected the field FNAME, you would be shown 10,000 first names.

Tables from Tables

The execution of a SELECT statement results in the creation of a new table, a table containing whatever columns were named in the SELECT statement and whatever fields within those columns were chosen by the query. The new table may be short-lived, existing only on your computer terminal screen; or, as we shall see later, the new table may be recorded permanently, as a written report or as a table within the database. In general, it should be kept in mind that the relational architecture contains only tables and produces only tables. A query which produces a single number nevertheless creates a new table, in this case a table of one column and one row.

2.2   The Where Clause

We know how to select all fields from a table. We know how to limit our field selection, how to choose just some fields for viewing. We now must find a way to limit our *record* selection, to pick and choose groups of records based upon some criteria. We can limit record selection with SQL's *where* clause:

```
SELECT BIRTH, LNAME, FNAME FROM PEOPLE
WHERE FNAME = 'Jennifer';
```

The word *where* in SQL serves to introduce one or more conditions, tests which each record in a table must meet and pass before it will be presented for viewing. In the above example only records which contain the characters "Jennifer" in the FNAME field will be selected. If no records contained that first name, then none would be returned. If all 10,000 of the people in our database had the first name "Jennifer" then our query would return 10,000 records.

With the where clause we arrive at the be-all and end-all of every database—the search. The storage of a great deal of data, in and of itself, is of little use; a dog-eared cardboard box can hold thousands upon thousands of facts. It is the ease of the *finding* which distinguishes (or should distinguish) a computer database from a "hard copy" collection of information. A search is always accompanied by some condition, some criteria, some values which will be used to determine which bits of information will be declared "a find" and which will not. The conditions stated in the where clause describe to the database program a search that it is to perform, and place limits upon field values, limits that will determine which records the search will return, which records will be "found" and which will not.

Note carefully the syntax: 1.) the word where is immediately followed by the name of a field; 2.) the field name is followed by the *type* of condition which it will have to meet; 3.) the condition type is followed by the *boundary* against which the field will be tried.

2.3   Conditions and Boundaries

The where clause may specify a variety of conditions which are to be met in carrying out a search. Each condition will be accompanied by certain *boundaries* which will be used in conjunction with the condition in order to test field values. Most conditions may be applied to both character fields and numeric fields. Conditions which may be applied to either type of field

WHERE CLAUSE CONDITIONS	
CONDITION	SYMBOL
Equal	=
Greater than	>
Less than	<
Greater than or equal to	>=
Less than or equal to	<=
Not equal	<>
Between	BETWEEN
Partial equality	LIKE
Equal to one item in a list	IN
Negation	NOT

Figure 2.2   Conditions.

will be accompanied by boundaries which can be applied to only one type of field. In other words, where clauses may be distinguished as to whether the field they refer to is of a numeric or character type.

Equal

The symbol is the equal sign:

where A = B

The condition of equality may be imposed upon character fields as well as upon numeric fields, but the boundary, that which the field must be equal to, is written with a different syntax depending upon whether the field being searched is character or numeric. A numeric boundary is written unadorned; a character boundary is expressed enclosed in single quotation marks:

SELECT NAME FROM S_SYSTEM WHERE DIAMETER = 75100;

SELECT FNAME FROM PEOPLE WHERE LNAME = 'Mallory';

Equality in a character field is "case sensitive"—an upper case 'M' is *not* the same as a lower case 'm'—and strings will match only if they match character for character.

TechNote: The ANSI standard declares that two strings are to be considered equal if the characters with the same ordinal position are equal. If the strings are of unequal length, the shorter string is to be

SELECT DIAMETER, DISTANCE, NAME FROM S_SYSTEM
WHERE DIAMETER < 10000;

DIAMETER	DISTANCE	NAME
3100	36	Mercury
7700	67	Venus
7927	93	Earth
4200	141	Mars
1500	3675	Pluto

Figure 2.3   A where clause using less than.

---

extended to the right with spaces until the strings are of equal length, and the comparison is to be made then.

Greater Than, Less Than

The symbols are > (greater than) and < (less than):
  where A > B (A greater than B)
  where A < B (A less than B)
The conditions greater than and less than may be used to test both numeric and character fields:

SELECT NAME FROM S_SYSTEM WHERE DIAMETER > 70000;

SELECT FNAME FROM PEOPLE WHERE LNAME < 'Mallory';

In character fields the greater than and less than conditions are determined by alphabetical order (upper case and lower case get somewhat thorny here—see the *Technote* below). The SELECT statement above would return any FNAME where the LNAME field began with any letter from 'A' to 'L', for each of these letters is "less than" the letter 'M'. It would likewise select a record where the LNAME field was 'Mallori', for this string is "less than" the string 'Mallory' (each letter is "equal" until we reach the last letter, and then the 'i' is less than the 'y', and so the entire string is "less then").

TechNote: Is a lower case 'm' less than or greater than an upper case 'M'? Is a lower case 'm' less than or greater than an upper case 'A'? This is to be determined, in the words of the ANSI standard, by the "implementor-defined collating sequence." In the real world it will be determined by whether your computer encodes characters with ASCII or EBCDIC. ASCII encoding is used by *all* personal computers and by most minicomputers. EBCDIC encoding is used on IBM mainframe computers. In ASCII any lower case letter is greater than any upper case letter. In EBCDIC any upper case letter is greater than any lower case letter. In ASCII the numeral characters 0-9 are less than any alphabetic character. In EBCDIC the numeral characters are greater than any alpha character.

Greater Than or Equal To, Less Than or Equal To

The symbols are >= (greater than or equal) and <= (less than or equal):
    where A >= B (A either greater than or equal to B)
    where A <= B (A either less than or equal to B)
These conditions may be used to test both numeric and character fields:

  SELECT NAME FROM S_SYSTEM WHERE DIAMETER >= 75100;

  SELECT FNAME FROM PEOPLE WHERE LNAME <= 'Mallory';

These conditions merely instruct the database program to make *two* comparisons during its search, and to declare success if either one is successful. The condition <= will cause a field to be checked as to whether it is less than the boundary *and* to be checked as to whether it is equal to the boundary. Note that these symbols are, syntactically, not mere combinations of the other symbols: You may *not* write '=>' or '=<'.

Not Equal

The symbol is <> (less than or greater than; i.e., not equal):
    where A <> B (A not equal to B)
This condition may be used to test both numeric and character fields:

  SELECT NAME FROM S_SYSTEM WHERE DIAMETER <> 75100;

  SELECT FNAME FROM PEOPLE WHERE LNAME <> 'Mallory';

The record will be selected only if the specified field is *not* equal to the specified boundary. It is required that the syntax be exactly as shown: It is *illegal* to write '><'.

  TechNote: Some computer programming languages use the symbol '!=' to mean "not equal." Before ANSI decided that the symbol for inequality would be '<>', some vendors of relational database products had already implemented systems using the syntax:
      where A != B
  If your system issues a complaint when you use '<>' for inequality, you might try using '!='.

Between

This condition is expressed with the words 'between' and 'and':

where A between B and C

This condition may be used to test both numeric and character fields:

    SELECT NAME FROM S_SYSTEM WHERE
    DIAMETER BETWEEN 7700 AND 75100;

    SELECT FNAME FROM PEOPLE WHERE LNAME
    BETWEEN 'Jones' AND 'Mallory';

The record will be selected if the specified field is greater than or equal to the first boundary *and* less than or equal to the second boundary. The between condition is equivalent to, and is in effect a shorthand way of saying:

where A >= B and A <= C

In fact it is entirely legal in SQL to rewrite the above SELECT statements thus:

    SELECT NAME FROM S_SYSTEM WHERE DIAMETER >= 7700
    AND DIAMETER <= 75100;

    SELECT FNAME FROM PEOPLE WHERE LNAME >= 'Jones'
    AND LNAME <= 'Mallory';

One might choose this longer form if one were very fond of typing.

Note that the lesser number or string *must* be specified first because the definition of BETWEEN assumes that the two values are specified in ascending order. The following statement would return no records:

    SELECT * FROM S_SYSTEM WHERE
    DIAMETER BETWEEN 75100 AND 7700;

If the two specified values are equal then the 'between' condition becomes a test for simple equality. The following statement would return only records which contained the string 'Mallory' in the LNAME field:

    SELECT * FROM PEOPLE WHERE
    LNAME BETWEEN 'Mallory' AND 'Mallory';

Like

This condition is expressed with the word 'like':

where A like 'B'

The ANSI standard declares that this condition may be used to test only character fields:

    SELECT FNAME FROM PEOPLE WHERE LNAME LIKE 'Jones';

SELECT * FROM S_SYSTEM WHERE NAME LIKE '%u%n%';

ID	NAME	DISTANCE	DIAMETER
1	Sun	0	865400
7	Saturn	887	75100
9	Neptune	2795	27700

Figure 2.4   A where clause using LIKE.

In the above SELECT statement the 'like' condition is doing nothing more than expressing equality; it is exactly equivalent to:

$$\text{where } A = B$$

The point and the power of the 'like' condition, however, is that it may express *partial* equality. It does so with the help of two special characters: the percent sign (%) and the underscore (_). These characters are both used as "wild cards," symbols which, in a search, will match *anything*. The percent sign will match any *one or more* character or characters and the underscore will match any *one* character. Each of the following SELECT statements will select any record having the character string "Jones" in its LNAME field:

1.) SELECT LNAME FROM PEOPLE WHERE LNAME LIKE '%';

2.) SELECT LNAME FROM PEOPLE WHERE LNAME LIKE 'J%';

3.) SELECT LNAME FROM PEOPLE WHERE LNAME LIKE 'J____';

4.) SELECT LNAME FROM PEOPLE WHERE LNAME LIKE '_____';

5.) SELECT LNAME FROM PEOPLE WHERE LNAME LIKE '%on%';

6.) SELECT LNAME FROM PEOPLE WHERE LNAME LIKE '__ne_';

7.) SELECT LNAME FROM PEOPLE WHERE LNAME LIKE '%_s';

8.) SELECT LNAME FROM PEOPLE WHERE LNAME LIKE '%o%e%';

Statement No. 1 will select *all* last names, including 'Jones'; statement No. 2 will select any last name, of any length, which begins with an upper case 'J'; statement No. 3 will select any last name containing five letters, the first of which is an upper case 'J'; statement No. 4 will select *all* last names containing five letters; statement No. 5 will select any last name containing the lower case letters 'on', in that order (the name would be selected if 'on' were the very first letters, if they were the very last letters, or if they were the *only* letters); statement No. 6 will select any last name containing five letters, with the letters 'ne' in the third and fourth positions; statement

No. 7 will select any last name which contains three *or more* characters and which ends in a lower case 's'; statement No. 8 will select any last name containing a lower case 'o' which is followed (immediately or at any other point in the string) by a lower case 'e'.

The like condition, with its mingling of characters and special search symbols, can be used to initiate subtle and interesting searches. Its possibilities need to be played with and explored.

Suppose a field contains the percent sign as one of its characters? How can you search for a percent sign? How can you search for an underscore? You will find that in some implementations of SQL you cannot perform such searches. The ANSI standard calls for allowing an *escape character* to be specified as part of the LIKE condition:

SELECT NAME FROM TABLES WHERE NAME LIKE 'S_%'
ESCAPE '\';

Here we have instructed the SQL interpreter to consider the backslash character, '\', as an escape character. An escape character, within a string that is to be searched for, means: look at the character immediately following the escape character and treat it as if it were a regular, ordinary character, even if it is one of the special search symbols. In the statement above, the underscore character, because it is preceded by an escape character, will be treated as a normal character and a search will be made for any name which begins with the two characters 'S_' (as does one of our table names, s_SYSTEM). Any single character may be specified as the escape character, but to avoid confusion (human confusion, that is) it is wise to use a character which does not normally appear in database character fields.

In

The condition IN specifies a list of items, each one of which will be compared for equality against the field which is being searched:

SELECT * FROM S_SYSTEM WHERE DISTANCE IN (36, 483, 3675);

SELECT * FROM PEOPLE WHERE LNAME IN
('Jones', 'Mallory', 'Weber', 'Smith');

SELECT NAME FROM MOONS WHERE PLANET
IN (1, 2, 3, 4);

The first statement above will return any record which contains in its DISTANCE field one of the numbers 36, 483, or 3675. The second statement will return any record which contains in its LNAME field one of the strings 'Mallory', 'Weber', or 'Smith'. The list specified in the 'in' condition may be as long as you wish to make it, or it may contain only one item. If an item specified in the list does not match any entry in the specified field, then no record will be returned for that item:

SELECT FNAME, LNAME FROM PEOPLE
WHERE LNAME IN ('Xquixteq');

The above statement would (probably) return no records.

Not

The negative condition, NOT, may be applied to the conditions LIKE, BE-
TWEEN, and IN. NOT is *always* used in conjunction with some other condition; it cannot be used alone. Its function is to stand the condition on its
head, to turn it about, to say: "take the following condition, and return to
me all records which do *not* meet the condition."

SELECT * FROM PEOPLE WHERE LNAME NOT LIKE 'Mallory';

The above statement will return every record which does *not* contain in its
LNAME field the string 'Mallory'.

SELECT NAME FROM S_SYSTEM WHERE DIAMETER
NOT BETWEEN 4200 and 32000;

The above statement will select the name of any planet which has a diameter
less than 4200 or *greater than* 32000.

SELECT * FROM PEOPLE WHERE LNAME
NOT IN ('Mallory', 'Jones');

The above statement will select records containing any last name *except*
'Mallory' or 'Jones'.

Is Null, Is Not Null

Records may be retrieved based upon the condition that a particular field
is or is not null. The following statement would select from our MONTH
table only that one week which did not contain a Thursday:

SELECT * FROM MONTH WHERE THU IS NULL;

Or we might want to look at all of the PEOPLE records which contained a
birth date:

SELECT * FROM PEOPLE WHERE BIRTH IS NOT NUILL;

2.4   Conditions Compounded

In discussing the where clause condition 'between' we noted that the statement:

where A between C and D

was equivalent to the statement:

where A >= C and A <= D

We thus introduced without discussion an important SQL construct, connectors. Connectors (in this case the word 'and') are the equivalent of

```
SELECT * FROM PEOPLE WHERE
(PROF IN ('Actress', 'Musician','Dancer'))
AND (STATE IN ('AZ', 'CO', 'FL'));
```

ID	FNAME	LNAME	PROF	BIRTH	CITY	STATE
6	Mary	DeMott	Actress	23-DEC-58	11	AZ
7	David	Dryden	Musician	03-FEB-49	14	CO
11	Mary	Bennett	Dancer	21-OCT-55	6	FL
13	Lance	Roberts	Dancer	11-JUL-50	11	AZ

Figure 2.5   Conditions grouped using AND.

English language conjunctions, and, as in English, they allow clauses to be multiplied, joined, and grouped. The connectors in SQL are 'and' and 'or'. A SELECT statement can be qualified by any number of where clauses using the SQL connectors.

Computer Logic

Computers do not deal in shades of gray. Things are true or false there. A compound statement is taken as a *whole* and evaluated as either true or false, even though it may contain parts which are true and parts which are false. The statement *Jennifer is a lawyer* is not compound and is therefore true or false depending upon whether its one clause is true or false. The statement *Jennifer is a lawyer and Jonathan is a cook* is compound and its parts are connected by the word *and*: the entire statement must therefore be counted as false if *either* of its claims is false. It will evaluate to true only if *both* clauses are true. The statement *Jonathan is a cook or Jennifer is a lawyer* is compound and its parts are connected with the word *or*: the entire statement will be counted as true if *either one* of its clauses is true. It will be set down as false only if *both* are false. The same is true no matter how many clauses are brought together with and: the statement *Jonathan is a cook and Jennifer is a lawyer and Michael is a pilot and Margaret is a doctor and...* is, all of it, entirely false if even one of the claims is false. The statement *Jonathan is a cook or Jennifer is a lawyer or Michael is a pilot or Margaret is a doctor or...* is, all of it, entirely true if even one of the claims is true.

And

In SQL, where clauses may be be strung together using 'and' just as clauses may be strung together in English. If we wanted to know the names of all

```
SELECT * PEOPLE WHERE PROF = 'Doctor'
OR STATE = 'AZ' OR STATE = 'FL';
```

ID	FNAME	LNAME	PROF	BIRTH	CITY	STATE
2	Margaret	Langer	Doctor	09-JUN-50	2	CA
6	Mary	DeMott	Actress	23-DEC-58	11	AZ
8	Elizabeth	Floyd	Programmer	05-SEP-57	6	FL
10	Mark	Feldman	Doctor	04-FEB-57	11	AZ
11	Mary	Bennett	Dancer	21-OCT-55	6	FL

Figure 2.6   Conditions grouped using OR.

the moons in the solar system which were greater than 1,000 kilometers in diameter *and* less than 500,000 kilometers from their planets, we could write:

```
SELECT NAME FROM MOONS WHERE DISTANCE < 500000
AND DIAMETER > 1000;
```

If we wanted to select from our *people* table everyone who lived in California, was a doctor, and was born before 1960, we could write:

```
SELECT FNAME, LNAME FROM PEOPLE WHERE STATE = 'CA'
AND PROF = 'Doctor' AND BIRTH < '01-JAN-60';
```

Or

Similarly, any number of alternative conditions may be imposed upon a search by connecting where clauses using the word 'or';

```
SELECT FNAME, LNAME FROM PEOPLE WHERE STATE = 'CA'
OR STATE = 'IL' OR PROF = 'Doctor'
OR PROF = 'Programmer';
```

The above statement will select anyone of any profession who lives in either California or Illinois; it will also select anyone who is either a doctor or a programmer, regardless of where they live. If we wanted a list of the moons in the solar system which either had a diameter of 3,000 or more kilometers *or* were 500,000 or more kilometers distant from their planets, we could write:

```
SELECT NAME FROM MOONS WHERE DISTANCE >= 500000
OR DIAMETER >= 3000;
```

And, Or Combinations

As long as we combine only 'and' clauses or only 'or' clauses, the truth or falsehood of the entire statement is easily evaluated: with 'and' clauses a statement is true only if *every* individual clause is true; with 'or' clauses a statement is true if *any* individual clause is true. But how will a computer evaluate conditions such as:

$$\text{where } A = 1 \text{ and } B = 2 \text{ or } C = 3$$
$$\text{where } A = 1 \text{ or } B = 2 \text{ and } C = 3$$
$$\text{where } A = 1 \text{ or } B = 2 \text{ and } C = 3 \text{ or } D = 4$$

The ANSI standard declares that "AND is applied before OR," which means, in a sense, that 'and' collects conditions more tightly, or "binds" them more strongly, than does 'or'. How the individual conditions above are "bound" may be shown using parentheses:

$$\text{where } (A = 1 \text{ and } B = 2) \text{ or } C = 3$$
$$\text{where } A = 1 \text{ or } (B = 2 \text{ and } C = 3)$$
$$\text{where } A = 1 \text{ or } (B = 2 \text{ and } C = 3) \text{ or } D = 4$$

The conditions grouped within parentheses will be evaluated as a *whole*, declared true or false as if they were a single condition. You can compose compound conditions far more complex than those above and, if you do, you may find it rather difficult trying to imagine where the parentheses might fall. Even if you did sort out all the groupings in your head, you might be unpleasantly surprised to find that your computer sorted it out differently. There is a very simple way to imagine how complex conditions will be grouped: *don't*. That is, *don't imagine it*, write it. Parentheses are a part of the SQL language. *Use them.* Wherever there is any possibility of ambiguity, write in the parentheses in order to make the statement clear:

```
SELECT NAME FROM MOONS WHERE
(DISTANCE >= 500000 AND DIAMETER >= 3000)
OR (DISTANCE <= 200000 AND DIAMETER >= 1000);

SELECT FNAME, LNAME FROM PEOPLE WHERE
(PROF = 'Doctor' AND BIRTH > '01-JAN-50')
AND (STATE IN ('NY', 'CA', 'FL'));
```

3. The Operators

The used key is always bright.

SELECT SUM(DONE) FROM TO_DO;

3.1   New Fields From Old

Numbers would be of some use if there were no addition, subtraction, multiplication, or division. But there would be no mathematics, no business. The huge edifice of modern science and industry is a great beehive of four symbols: '+', '−', 'x', and '/'. These are OPERATORS, signs which command numbers to combine, and which insist that results be brought forth. The vast array of all the numbers is brought to order and made to do work by the operators.

Databases can easily comprise thousands or even millions of records, with each record itself containing a number of fields. If our access to this information were limited to a full listing or to various partial lists, we would be in the same position as a mathematician faced with the integers and not armed with any operators. SQL's toolbox contains a useful collection of operators, allowing fields to be combined and acted upon in various ways. The results of such operations are, in effect, new fields, fields which are not held in storage within the database, but which can be brought forth, or created, at any time. If we add field A to field B we get a value, call it field C, which is not written upon our computer's storage device, but which is there nevertheless, to be retrieved and used.

SQL OPERATORS	
OPERATOR	SYMBOL
Addition	+
Subtraction	−
Multiplication	*
Division	/
Count	COUNT
Maximum	MAX
Minimum	MIN
Average	AVG
Sum	SUM

Figure 3.1   The operators.

DesignNote: The arsenal of operators is of use not merely *after* the database is brimming with information; their existence and abilities should be weighed and considered before any decision is made as to what bits of information will be permanently stored in database fields. In order to preserve storage space, no information that can be *calculated* should be stored. If we decide to allot a field for a person's birthdate, then it would simply be wasted storage to allot a field for that person's age. Given the birthdate and today's date, the age can be calculated at any time (to say nothing of the risk involved in storing elusive things like age, which tend to change from day to day).

3.2   The Tool Box

SQL allows for the four arithmetic operations: addition, subtraction, multiplication and division. It also provides special operators which allow the user to count selected fields; to find the lowest or highest of the fields selected; to find the average of the selected fields; to find the sum of the selected fields. The arithmetic operators may be combined:

select $((A + B) - C)$ from table where ...
select $(2 * (A + B))$ from table where ...
select $((A - B) / 2)$ from table where ...

The special operators may be used in combination with the arithmetic operators:

select $max((A + B) - C) ...$
select $avg(A + B) ...$
select $sum((A - B) / 2) ...$

SELECT WHEN, WHAT, (SPENT — TAX) FROM ADVERT;

WHEN	WHAT	(SPENT—TAX)
31-DEC-86	New Year's Party	200.47
05-JAN-87	Catalog	307.99
10-JAN-87	Postage	44.65
11-JAN-87	Telephone	95.71
15-JAN-87	Travel - Atlanta	412.09

Figure 3.2   Creating a new field with subtraction.

The operators may be combined flexibly and creatively to fill a wide range of database needs.

Addition and Subtraction

The symbols for addition and subtraction are '+' and '−', and may be applied only to numeric fields. Numeric fields may be added to or subtracted from other numeric fields. Constant values may be added to or subtracted from numeric fields. If the telephone company were proposing an additonal one dollar processing charge per bill and if we wanted to look at what our bills would have been last year if such a charge had been in effect, we could query:

    SELECT WHEN, (SPENT + 1.00) FROM ADVERT
    WHERE WHAT = 'Telephone';

If we wanted to know how much of those hypothetical charges would have gone to the telephone company itself, rather than to taxes, we could query:

    SELECT WHEN, ((SPENT − TAX) + 1.00) FROM ADVERT
    WHERE WHAT = 'Telephone';

Multiplication and Division

The symbols for multiplication and division are '*' and '/', and may be applied only to numeric fields. Fields may be multiplied or divided by constant values, or by other fields. If we wanted to compare the cost of a flat 5% tax rate to the taxes which we actually paid, we might query:

    SELECT WHEN, WHAT, TAX, ((SPENT   TAX) * 0.05)
    FROM ADVERT;

```
SELECT MAX(DIAMETER), MIN(DISTANCE) FROM S_SYSTEM
WHERE NAME <> 'Sun';
```

MAX(DIAMETER)	MIN(DISTANCE)
88700	36

```
SELECT MAX(NAME), MIN(STATE) FROM CITY;
```

MAX(NAME)	MIN(STATE)
Tucson	AZ

Figure 3.3   Finding the greatest and the least.

If we wanted to view the diameters of the solar system's moons in miles rather than kilometers, knowing that there are 1.6 kilometers per mile, we could query:

```
SELECT NAME, (DIAMETER / 1.6) FROM MOONS;
```

If we wanted to know the diameters of the planets in kilometers, rather than miles, we could query:

```
SELECT NAME, (DIAMETER * 1.6) FROM S_SYSTEM;
```

The arithmetic operators, combined with parentheses, can be compounded to any degree of complexity. How far you will be able to go with such arithmetic acrobatics will depend upon the limitations of your particular database implementation, but all things are theoretically possible:

$$\text{select } (((A + B) - C) * ((D / E) + (F - G)))\ldots$$

Maximum and Minimum

The SQL operators which seek out the greatest or the least value within selected fields use the symbols MAX and MIN, and may be employed upon both numeric and character fields. With numeric fields these operators, of course, return simply the highest or lowest number among those selected. With character fields, these operators return the field value which is highest or lowest according to the manner in which character values are ordered in a particular database implementation. The manner of ordering characters is usually dependent upon the particular computer upon which the application is running. Most computers use either ASCII or EBCDIC to

SELECT COUNT(NAME) FROM MOONS;

<u>COUNT(NAME)</u>

24

SELECT AVG(DISTANCE), AVG(DIAMETER) FROM S_SYSTEM
WHERE NAME <> 'Sun';

<u>AVG(DISTANCE)</u>   <u>AVG(DIAMETER)</u>

1106.66   27547.44

Figure 3.4   Counting and finding averages.

---

encode character values (see the *TechNote* on page 15), and this code will
determine how character fields are ordered.

If we wished to determine the greatest single expenditure of the advertising department, excluding tax, we could query:

SELECT MAX(SPENT − TAX) FROM ADVERT;

If a scientist were investigating possible relationships between the diameters
and orbital distances of the moons in our solar system, and wanted to find
the smallest ratio of distance to diameter, she could query:

SELECT MIN(DISTANCE / DIAMETER) FROM MOONS;

Count

The SQL operator which takes a head count of fields is COUNT, and may be
used to count both numeric and character fields. This operator simply runs
down the named column and ticks off one count for each field in that column
which meets whatever where clause conditions you may have specified; it
then returns the accumulated count to you. To count all of the objects in
our Solar System table we could write:

SELECT COUNT(NAME) FROM S_SYSTEM;

To count only the proper planets we might write:

SELECT COUNT(NAME) FROM S_SYSTEM WHERE DISTANCE > 0;

We could find how many times the advertising department paid a tax with
the following query:

SELECT COUNT(SPENT) FROM ADVERT WHERE TAX > 0;

SELECT AVG(BUDGET — SPENT) FROM ADVERT
WHERE BUDGET IS NOT NULL;

AVG(BUDGET - SPENT)
$\overline{\hspace{3cm}}$
20.23

SELECT SUM(SPENT) FROM ADVERT
WHERE WHAT LIKE '%Lunch%';

SUM(SPENT)
$\overline{\hspace{2cm}}$
52.88

Figure 3.5   Average over budget and total for lunches.

Just as we can select all rows from a table by using the asterisk, so may we use the asterisk in order to get a count of how many rows there are in a table:

SELECT COUNT(*) FROM PEOPLE;

SELECT COUNT(*) FROM MOONS;

Sum

We can command SQL to add up the values in all selected numeric fields (we cannot add character fields) with the operator SUM. This operator will be the workhorse in any database which records accounts payable, accounts receivable, and such. It will be used to obtain subtotals and grand totals:

SELECT SUM(SPENT) FROM ADVERT;

SELECT SUM(SPENT) FROM ADVERT WHERE WHAT = 'Telephone';

SELECT SUM(SPENT) FROM ADVERT WHERE
WHEN BETWEEN '01-JUN-87' AND '30-JUN-87';

DesignNote: When designing tables which are to record financial or numeric data, you should decide which fields to include and which to exclude with an eye toward what sort of summary information you will want to be able to extract from your data. If you will want a separate sum of how much sales tax was paid, then tax paid must in some way be captured in your table. In designing tables you must also be aware of the form in which the data will be given to whoever

SELECT COUNT(NAME), AVG(DISTANCE), AVG(DIAMETER)
FROM MOONS WHERE PLANET = 6;

COUNT(NAME)	AVG(DISTANCE)	AVG(DIAMETER)
9	2315666.67	1294.11

SELECT COUNT(NAME), AVG(DISTANCE / 1.6), AVG(DIAMETER / 1.6)
FROM MOONS WHERE PLANET = 6;

COUNT(NAME)	AVG(DISTANCE/1.6)	AVG(DIAMETER/1.6)
9	1447291.67	808.82

Figure 3.6   The moons of Saturn, in kilometers and miles.

---

will be doing data entry. The person should not be required to do any calculations; that is SQL's job. In our ADVERT table we might have used fields SUBTOTAL and TAX rather than SPENT and TAX. We could then always calculate 'spent' by adding SUBTOTAL and TAX. But what if a bill had only a total? Our data entry person can calculate tax, if he must, or it could be left to be calculated later, by SQL (as should be done). If the fields to be entered were SUBTOTAL and TAX, then the data entry fellow would have no choice—he would *have to* calculate both.

Average

An operator with the symbol AVG allows us to take the sum of the selected fields and divide that sum by the count of the selected fields, which is to say it allows us to obtain an average of the selected fields. The operator is really a shorthand way of doing what we could do by combining the SUM and COUNT operators:

SELECT AVG(DISTANCE) FROM MOONS;

We could achieve exactly the same results as the above query by writing:

SELECT (SUM(DISTANCE) / COUNT(DISTANCE)) FROM MOONS;

3.3   Distinct

SQL allows for the elimination of duplicate values within a query by using the word DISTINCT. The word may be used in conjunction with the oper-

SELECT COUNT (DISTINCT PLANET) FROM MOONS;

COUNT(DISTINCT PLANET)

7

Figure 3.7   Using DISTINCT to find how many planets have moons.

---

ators. The word should immediately precede the name of the field being selected:

SELECT DISTINCT CITY FROM PEOPLE;

The above query would tell us how many different cities were represented in our PEOPLE table. Similarly, we could find the number of different states represented in the CITY table with the following query:

SELECT DISTINCT STATE FORM CITY;

We could discover how many different professions were represented in our PEOPLE table by writing:

SELECT DISTINCT PROF FORM PEOPLE;

3.4   Single-value Queries

The operators MIN, MAX, COUNT, SUM, and AVG all return a single value, no matter how many rows of a table the SELECT statement may actually examine, no matter how many fields the where clause may choose. Queries which return a single value return, in effect, a table of just one column and one row. We must consider here the effect of combining, in a single SELECT statement, queries which must return a single value with queries which may return many values. Since any given field in a record may contain only a single value, such queries are disallowed:

SELECT NAME, AVG(DISTANCE) FORM MOONS;

SELECT WHEN, WHAT, SUM(SPENT) FROM ADVERT;

The difficulty is that the above SELECT statements must, as must all SELECT statements, either return a table or nothing at all. The NAME portion of the first statement will return a row for each row in the MOONS table, but the AVG(DISTANCE) portion of the statement can return only a single value, a single row. The resulting table would contain only a single row, but we would have multiple values for one of its fields, the NAME field. This is not allowed.

3.5   Operators and Nulls

A null is an unknown. A field which contains a null is a field with contents which are unknown. What will SQL do if we ask it to perform some arithmetic operation with a null field? It will return a null. No matter what the arithmetic expression may be, if a null field is involved, the result of the expression will be null. *Any arithmetic expression containing a null as one of its elements will return a null.* The BUDGET field in our ADVERT table contains a number of nulls (some things are not budgeted). The following expressions would return a null for each null field in the BUDGET column:

SELECT (BUDGET + 1.00) FROM ADVERT;

SELECT (BUDGET − 1.00) FROM ADVERT;

SELECT (BUDGET * 0.5) FROM ADVERT;

SELECT (BUDGET / 2) FROM ADVERT;

SELECT (BUDGET − SPENT) FROM ADVERT;

The operators MIN, MAX, COUNT, SUM, and AVG all *ignore* null fields. MIN and MAX will find the minimum or maximum value of those fields which are not null. COUNT will count only fields which are not null, so that the expression COUNT(BUDGET) would not return the number of rows in the ADVERT table, but only the number of rows in which BUDGET was not null. SUM will add together only fields which are not null, and AVG will average only those fields which are not null.

> *DesignNote:* All design is foresight. Knowing what you have, you must be able to see what you *will have* tomorrow, if you do thus and such today. Knowing that operators like COUNT and AVG will ignore null fields, you should foresee that allowing null vlaues in numeric fields may result in inaccurate calculations of averages. We will see later on that we may disallow null values in particular columns when we create a table. This should be done for any column which will be used to generate summary data.

Since the COUNT operator ignores null fields, is there any way to determine how many fields in a particular column are null? The following query will not work:

SELECT COUNT(BUDGET) FROM ADVERT
WHERE BUDGET IS NULL;

The query will return zero. Since COUNT ignores null fields, and since the query is selecting *only* null fields, COUNT will count nothing, leaving a result of zero. The following query will tell us how many expenses were made which were not budgeted:

```
SELECT COUNT(SPENT) FROM ADVERT
WHERE BUDGET IS NULL;
```

The SPENT field cannot be null. The above query will select each row which contains a null BUDGET field, and the COUNT operator will tick off one count for each row selected, since it will always find the SPENT field occupied. The result will be an accurate count of those rows which contain a null BUDGET field.

3.6   Beyond the Standard

Commercial implementations of SQL have gone far beyond the ANSI standard in stocking the tool chest with operators. Additonal operators will undoubtedly be added to the standard in the future. Whatever implementation you are working with, you will probably find that you have more to work with than MIN, MAX, COUNT, SUM, and AVG. We will mention only a few of the possibilities here. You may find that they do or do not exist in your database, or that similar operators, spelled differently, exist, or that similarly spelled operators behave differently.

Effective searches for particular letter patterns within text fields will be difficult, if not impossible, without operators such as UPPER and LOWER. UPPER would convert all characters in a field to upper case, and LOWER would convert to lower case. If you needed to search through hundreds of lengthy text fields for the word "periwinkle" you would probably want fields to be selected if they contained "periwinkle," "Periwinkle," "PERIWINKLE," or even a typo such as "PeriwINkle." With operators such as UPPER and LOWER, searching for every possibility can be done in a single statement:

```
SELECT UPPER(text) FROM table WHERE
text LIKE '%PERIWINKLE%';
```

The operator UPPER would cause every letter in each selected field to be converted to upper case, *before* a search was made for the word "PERIWINKLE." Any form of the word would have been converted to upper case and would therefore match the search word. We would get exactly the same result if we used the operator LOWER and the search word in lower case:

```
SELECT LOWER(text) FROM table WHERE text LIKE '%periwinkle%';
```

It is often useful to know how long a character field is. Such information is often needed when writing reports. The operator which reports such information is usually called LENGTH. The following statement would tell us how many characters there were in each of our text fields:

```
SELECT LENGTH(text) FROM table;
```

Operators and Dates

Since the ANSI standard does not provide for date field types, it naturally does not provide any operators for manipulating dates. Again, commercial implementions of SQL go well beyond the standard (they existed long before the standard) and some provide numerous operators for dissecting and combining date fields in various ways.

Some of the date field operations which have been implemented are listed below:

Day arithmetic—any number of days may be added to or subtracted from a date, the result being a new date:

    SELECT (10/10/87 + 45)...;

    SELECT (10/10/87 − 60)...;

Two dates may be subtracted, giving the number of days between them:

    SELECT (10/10/87 − 2/21/87)...;

Month arithmetic—months may be added to or subtracted from a date, yielding a new date:

    SELECT MONTHS_ADD(10/10/87 + 6)...;

The above function provides addition or subtraction by adding either positive or negative numbers to the date. Dates may be subtracted, yielding the number of months between:

    SELECT MONTHS_BETWEEN(1/2/86, 7/12/87)...;

Next date—the date of a particular day of the week following a given date may be found:

    SELECT NEXT_DATE(9/14/87, 'MONDAY')...;

The above query would return the date of the Monday following 9/14/87. We might want to schedule next year's board meeting for a date as close to this year's, while making sure that the selected date did not fall on a Saturday, Sunday, or the Monday or Friday of a holiday weekend:

    SELECT NEXT_DATE
    ((MONTHS_ADD(BOARD_DATE + 12)), 'WEDNESDAY')...;

TechNote: The programming which stands behind date manipulation is not at all trivial. When adding days to a date, a program must know the maximum number of days within each month, and must know whether or not any of the years involved is a leap year.

A number of other tools could be added for date manipulation. In your particular SQL implementation you may find that your tool box contains more than those listed above, or you may find that it contains no date operators at all.

4. The Ordering of Information

A good carpenter does not complain of his tools.

SELECT SUM(RESULTS) FROM PROJECTS
GROUP BY END_DATE ORDER BY PRIORITY;

4.1 Passive Observer

We have found that, with the names of tables and their fields, we can,
using very simple sentences, obtain all of the information contained in those
tables. We can view every field in every record. We can view selected fields
from selected records. We can set the order in which the fields will be
presented to us. We can have fields acted upon by some constant value,
through addition, subtraction, multiplication, or division. We can even
command fields to combine and to bring forth sums and averages. When
we consider that a database may well contain dozens of tables, holding many
thousands of records and fields, it may well seem that our simple sentences
have empowered us with great authority in this realm, this database.

In fact we are still just passive observers. We can look, but our latitude
for *acting* is limited. We can manipulate the way in which fields are to be
displayed, and have our manipulations ripple through the display of many
records, but in the end those records will be presented in whatever order
they are found in; SQL will step down the table, from record to record,
testing each against whatever conditions we have set, and retrieving or
discarding each, as it is found. As yet we have no power over that larger
structure, the record, the row. We cannot say, "Take this group of records

SELECT * FROM CITY WHERE NAME < 'M'
ORDER BY NAME ASC;

ID	NAME	STATE
20	Albany	NY
7	Atlanta	GA
17	Bismarck	ND
8	Boise	ID
25	Buffalo	NY
12	Carson City	NV
3	Chicago	IL
14	Denver	CO
5	Durham	NC
11	Flagstaff	AZ
15	Honolulu	HI
13	Lansing	MI
10	Lexington	KY

Figure 4.1   Order a portion of the CITY table by city name.

and display them here, and take that group and display them there." Soon
we will have the sentences to do such things.

We might perhaps imagine a database which was fixed, which had completed its collection of information, and had had all of that information verified. But that information could be stored in just the order in which everyone at all times would want to see it, that we cannot imagine.

4.2   Orders and Groups

SQL provides two powerful tools for the gathering of records. We can command that all selected records be presented to us in some particular order. We can then issue the same command with a second scheme of order. We can then choose another, and yet another, order, repeatedly rearranging and regrouping the records in our tables, seeing the data in different ways, from different vantage points, with altering emphasis. In this way the same bed of data can be made to grow different flowers of information, and the inquirer may, again and again, see there things which she had not seen before.

You will acquire some feel for the power of this simple procedure if

SELECT STATE, NAME FROM CITY WHERE STATE < 'M'
ORDER BY STATE, NAME ASC;

STATE	NAME
AZ	Flagstaff
AZ	Tucson
CA	San Francisco
CA	San Jose
CO	Denver
FL	Miami
FL	Tampa
GA	Atlanta
GA	Macon
HI	Honolulu
ID	Boise
ID	Moscow
IL	Chicago
KY	Lexington

Figure 4.2   Order the CITY table by city name within state.

---

you imagine an everyday object and what you can and cannot do with it. Imagine having a telephone book open before you; then imagine that you have snapped your fingers, and suddenly all of the thousands of listings are arranged by the person's first name, rather than the last (page after page of "Mary, ..."); then another snap, and all are listed by address; another snap, and the lising is by phone number. Such magical transformations become commonplace with SQL's ordering tool.

SQL also allows records to be grouped. We can command that, as records are selected, they be dropped into various pigeonholes, and that we be presented with summary information about each pigeonhole. We might snap our fingers and be told how many people in the phone book fell into the 'Mary' pigeonhole; how many fell into the 'Feldman' pigeonhole; how many were listed for some particular address; or the number of people listed for *every* separate address.

Selecting ordered records and groups of records does not in any way affect the database itself, the data in its storage bins. Nothing is *physically* moved, no table is altered. Grouping and ordering merely allow us to rear-

```
SELECT * FROM STATE WHERE
NAME BETWEEN 'Ca' AND 'Oz'
ORDER BY NAME DESC;
```

NAME	STATE
Oregon	OR
North Dakota	NC
North Carolina	NC
New York	NY
New Mexico	NM
New Hampshire	NH
Nevada	NV
Michigan	MI
Massachusetts	MA
Kentucky	KY
Illinois	IL
Idaho	ID
Hawaii	HI
Georgia	GA
Florida	FL
Dist. of Columbia	DC
Colorado	CO
California	CA

Figure 4.3   Order a portion of the STATE table by state name.

range data *as it is shown to us.* We can arrange and rearrange, and again rearrange, in a playful, exploratory way, without altering the database.

4.3   Ordering

The SQL command which causes selected records to be displayed in a selected order is ORDER BY. The command should follow the 'WHERE clause' within the SELECT statement, or immediately follow the table name if no 'WHERE clause' is specified:

SELECT field FROM table WHERE ... ORDER BY ... ;

SELECT field FROM table ORDER BY ... ;

Selected records may be ordered by any field. They may be ordered by a text field or by a numeric field. The order may be ascending (lowest number or letter first) or descending (highest number or letter first). SQL specifies ascending or descending with the abbreviations ASC and DESC. The order specification should immediately follow the order by clause:

SELECT field FROM table ORDER BY ... ASC;

SELECT field FROM table ORDER BY ... DESC;

If neither ASC nor DESC is specified, SQL will order the records in ascending order.

Records may be ordered by any number of fields in combination. The fields to be used are separated by commas in the order by clause:

SELECT * FROM PEOPLE ORDER BY LNAME, FNAME;

In the above statement, records would be presented with last names in alphabetical order *and*, for each last name which appeared more than once, with first names in alphabetical order also. See Figure 4.2 for an example of ordering with multiple fields.

> *TechNote:* The SELECT statement in figure 4.3 selects fields between 'Ca' and 'Oz', *not* between 'C' and 'O'. Had we selected between 'C' and 'O' we would have gotten no names beginning with the letter 'O', because the BETWEEN operator resolves to '>= C and <= O'. None of the names in the table are equal to simply the letter 'O', and so we should have gotten no 'O' names. 'Oz' insures that we will see any name beginning with 'O' which is not "greater than" the combination 'Oz'. We could have been even more certain of including all 'O' names by setting our boundary to 'Ozzzzzzz'. Again it should be stressed that upper case and lower case letters very much affect the outcome of this sort of search. See the TechNote on page 15 and the discussion of UPPER and LOWER on page 34.

4.4   Grouping

The SQL command which causes records to be grouped and the groups to be considered as a whole is GROUP BY. The command should follow the 'WHERE clause' within the SELECT statement, or immediately follow the table name if no 'WHERE clause' is specified:

SELECT COUNT(field) FROM table WHERE ... GROUP BY ...;

SELECT COUNT(field) FROM table GROUP BY ...;

if an ORDER BY clause is specified as well as a GROUP BY clause, the ORDER BY clause should be specified last.

```
SELECT STATE, COUNT(NAME) FROM CITY
WHERE STATE > 'L'
GROUP BY STATE ORDER BY COUNT(NAME);
```

STATE	COUNT(NAME)
MI	1
NC	1
ND	1
NH	1
NM	1
NV	1
OR	1
RI	1
WA	2
NY	3

Figure 4.4   Counting within groups and ordering by that count.

```
SELECT PLANET, MAX(DISTANCE), MIN(DISTANCE),
MAX(DIAMETER), MIN(DIAMETER) FROM MOONS
GROUP BY PLANET ORDER BY MAX(DIAMETER);
```

PLANET	MAX(DIS)	MIN(DIS)	MAX(DIA)	MIN(DIA)
4	23490	9354	27	15
9	17000	17000	1200	1200
7	586000	130000	1620	320
3	384000	384000	3480	3480
8	5562000	355000	4000	500
6	12954000	186000	5150	205
5	1880000	422000	5276	3126

Figure 4.5   Maximum and minimum values for each group.

```
SELECT STATE, COUNT(NAME) FROM CITY
WHERE CITY > 'L'
GROUP BY STATE ORDER BY STATE;
```

STATE	COUNT(NAME)
MI	1
NC	1
ND	1
NH	1
NM	1
NV	1
NY	3
OR	1
RI	1
WA	2

Figure 4.6   Counting records within certain groups.

```
SELECT field, COUNT(field) FROM table
GROUP BY field ORDER BY field;
```

More than a single field may be specified within the GROUP BY clause:

```
SELECT NAME, STATE FROM CITY GROUP BY NAME, STATE;
```

Note that the above SELECT statement would have no effect upon our CITY table because it has only one record for each NAME, STATE pair. Multiple field grouping would be meaningful with more complex tables.

Single-value Selects

When a GROUP BY clause is used in a SELECT statement, the fields specified in the SELECT clause must evaluate to a *single value for each group.* As we have noted before, the result of a SELECT statememt is a new table. Within any given row of our new table, each field may contain only a single value. If we write our SELECT statement so that it would produce more than one value for a single field, SQL will present us with an error message:

```
SELECT NAME, STATE FROM CITY GROUP BY STATE;
```

The above SELECT statement is illegal. As we know, some states in the CITY table appear more than once, each coupled with a different city name. Since the above statement is grouped by state, it will produce only a single

```
SELECT STATE, COUNT(NAME) FROM CITY
GROUP BY STATE HAVING COUNT(NAME) > 1
ORDER BY COUNT(NAME);
```

STATE	COUNT(NAME)
AZ	2
CA	2
FL	2
GA	2
ID	2
WA	2
NY	3

Figure 4.7   Using HAVING to select only certain groups.

---

row for each state name. But some of those rows would contain more than a single value in the NAME field. This is not allowed.

Having

We can use the GROUP BY clause to acquire summary information about various groups within a table, such as the number of records within each group, the sum of certain fields within each group, etc. Suppose that we wanted to be shown only certain groups, only groups whose summary information met certain criteria. We cannot use a WHERE clause to select groups:

```
SELECT STATE, COUNT(NAME) FROM CITY
WHERE COUNT(NAME) > 1 GROUP BY STATE;
```

The above statement is illegal. The WHERE clause condition is used by SQL to test individual records, and either select or reject each. The WHERE clause in the above statement refers to the summary information which will be produced by the GROUP BY clause, and is therefore disallowed as it is written above. We can specify conditions and boundaries to be used with the GROUP BY clause by using the SQL clause HAVING. The statement below will accomplish what we tried to do in the previous, illegal, statement:

```
SELECT STATE, COUNT(NAME) FROM CITY
GROUP BY STATE HAVING COUNT(NAME) > 1;
```

The HAVING clause is merely a means of specifying conditions which groups of records must meet, just as the WHERE clause is used to specify conditions which individual records must meet.

5. Joining Tables

*Better to wear out
than to rust out.*

SELECT DAY FROM LIFE
WHERE ACTIVITY = 'FULL';

5.1   The Birth of Design

We have constructed sentences which permit us to acquire any record or group of records within any table, and to order those records and groups. We will now go further, and devise sentences which will allow us to bring together the largest structures of the relational architecture, the tables themselves. We will find that with a select statement we can create a new table which consists of one column from this table, one column from that, and another column from yet a third table. We will specify that a record from one table is to be selected only if one of its fields is equal to one of the fields in a record from a second table.

   With this expanded capability we must widen our vision and begin to look upon the database, the collection of tables, as one cooperating whole. We will see that tables must be shaped so that they may participate in the larger, interconnected mechanism, the database. We will see that parts of tables, or, in some cases, whole tables, are best reduced to cryptic numeric tags so that they may, while consuming the least possible space, efficiently connect to information in other tables. We will find the dilemma and the delight of all learning: You cannot design a single table well unless you have first designed many, and you cannot design many without first designing one.

5.2   Full Field Names

If we are going to select, with one statement, fields from a number of different tables, we must have some way of specifying particular fields without ambiguity. A number of our tables contain a field called NAME. We could select, within one statement, a number of these NAME fields. But how would SQL know which NAME field to associate with which table?

Although field names may be duplicated in different tables, a database can never contain duplicate table names. We can uniquely identify any field in our database by specifying the table name along with the field name. In SQL a full field name is formed by appending the table name to the field name, using a period as the connector. The full names of all the fields in the MOONS table are:

MOONS.PLANET

MOONS.NAME

MOONS.DISTANCE

MOONS.DIAMETER

Full field names may be used wherever field names are acceptable. The asterisk may be combined with a table name to specify "all fields." A few of the SQL statements already used in this book are repeated below using full field names:

SELECT MONTH.* FROM MONTH;

SELECT PEOPLE.LNAME FROM PEOPLE
WHERE LNAME <> 'Mallory';

SELECT CITY.NAME, CITY.STATE FROM CITY
ORDER BY CITY.STATE;

Using full field names in statements such as those above is simply an exercise in extra typing. Since only one table is specified, SQL will have no difficulty deciding which table to look to for the specified fields. Full field names need be specified only where field name ambiguity may exist, only when two or more tables, containing identical field names, are accessed in a single select statement.

5.3   The Join

Any select statement which requests fields from two or more tables is called a JOIN. The word is also used to refer to the table which results from the select statement. Joins and the statements which produce them are the

SELECT S_SYSTEM.NAME, PEOPLE.FNAME FROM S_SYSTEM, PEOPLE;

S_SYSTEM.NAME	PEOPLE.FNAME
Sun	Jennifer
Sun	Margaret
Sun	Jonathan
⋮	⋮
Pluto	Jennifer
Pluto	Margaret
Pluto	Jonathan
⋮	⋮

Figure 5.1   All possible combinations.

---

real workhorses of the relational architecture. It is a rare database which can capture all that it needs in one single table. Rarely will the tables in a database be so unrelated as to require no joins. Nor *should* these things be true. If you do not have a variegated and malleable collection of tables, whose various joins can illuminate and expand the information they hold, then you are not really using the relational architecture.

In a select statement which chooses from more than a single table, the table names are listed, separated by commas, just as we list multiple fields:

SELECT table1.field1, table2.field2 FROM table1, table2 WHERE ...;

Combinations

To demonstrate the mechanism which underlies the join, let's begin with something silly:

SELECT S_SYSTEM.NAME, PEOPLE.FNAME
FROM S_SYSTEM, PEOPLE;

The two tables are unrelated, and even were they related, we have expressed no WHERE clause which might tell SQL *how* they are related. The statement, however, is perfectly legal. What will SQL do? Since it has been given no clue as to how we wish NAME and FNAME to be joined, it will produce a table which joins them *in every possible way*. It will give us a table containing records with two fields, NAME and FNAME. The first record will join 'Sun' with 'Jennifer', the second will join 'Mercury' with 'Jennifer', and so on. When every planet name has been joined with 'Jennifer', then

```
SELECT CITY.NAME, PEOPLE.FNAME, PEOPLE.LNAME
FROM CITY, PEOPLE WHERE CITY.ID = PEOPLE.CITY;
```

CITY.NAME	PEOPLE.FNAME	PEOPLE.LNAME
New York	Jennifer	Mallory
San Francisco	Margaret	Langer
Chicago	Jonathan	Drake
Lexington	David	Braverman
Lansing	Daisy	Escher
Flagstaff	Mary	DeMott
Denver	David	Dryden
Miami	Elizabeth	Floyd
Chicago	Connie	DeMarco
Flagstaff	Mark	Feldman
Miami	Mary	Bennett
Lexington	Martha	Redwood
Flagstaff	Lance	Roberts

Figure 5.2   Using join columns.

---

every planet name will be joined with 'Margaret', and then they will all be joined with 'Jonathan', until every planet name has been joined to every person name. Our silly statement says, in effect, "Show me every possible way in which these two items might be combined," and that is precisely what we will be shown.

Join Columns

Tables which can be meaningfully combined will contain JOIN COLUMNS, columns which SQL can use in order to associate a particular record from one table to some record from another table. We can now see why many of our tables contain a column (usually called ID) which can be used to assign a number to each record. It is these numbers which become the join columns, which are written into the join columns of other tables, thus linking records one-to-one. We numbered each planet in our S_SYSTEM table, so that we could tie each moon in our MOONS table to its respective planet, by writing the planet's number into the PLANET field in the MOONS table.

   TechNote: Why use numbers? Why create a separate field, ID, in order to identify a planet's name? Why not just use the planet's name? In a relational database implemention, as in any computer application, the storage of numbers will, in general, require a great deal less space than the storage of character strings. Numbers up to five digits in length can be stored in the space required by only two characters. To store a number for each planet, and a similar number for each moon, of course, requires storage space. But to have stored the string 'Saturn' for each of its nine moons would have required a great deal more space.

DesignNote: Some join columns occur naturally, and will occur in tables without much thought being given to them. We have used the two character state name abbreviations as join columns in a few of our tables. Most join columns, however, must be foreseen and created specifically as join columns. The two important factors to be considered in selecting or designing a join column are *length* and *uniqueness*. Since the value in a join column may potentially be repeated numerous times throughout the database, linking many records to the record containing the join column value, the value should be one which will occupy little space, one which is, in a word, short. The value in a join column should also be *unique within its table*. The value need not be unique across the entire database, since the table name will always be a part of the field identifier. But if a field is to be used for joining records from other tables, the value in that field should appear in no other field within the column containing that field.

5.4   Alias Names

SQL allows the writer of a select statement to assign new names to tables within the select statement. These stand-in names are commonly known as ALIAS names. The ANSI standard refers to them as CORRELATION names. A table alias remains in effect, and is recognized by the database, only while the select statement containing it is executing. An alias name is specified by simply following the table name with whatever alias you wish to use:

    SELECT S_SYSTEM.NAME, PEOPLE.FNAME
    FROM S_SYSTEM ALIAS_A, PEOPLE ALIAS_B;

In the above statement we have given the alias 'ALIAS_A' to the table 'S_SYSTEM' and the alias 'ALIAS_B' to the table 'PEOPLE'. In doing so, we have accomplished nothing because, although we assigned the alias names, we did not *use* them. Alias names can be used, among other things, to reduce the amount of typing needed in a select statement:

    SELECT CITY.NAME, PEOPLE.FNAME, PEOPLE.LNAME
    FROM CITY C, PEOPLE P WHERE C.ID = P.CITY;

```
SELECT A.FNAME, A.LNAME, A.STATE, B.FNAME, B.LNAME
FROM PEOPLE A, PEOPLE B WHERE
(A.STATE = B.STATE) AND (A.ID > B.ID)
ORDER BY A.STATE;
```

A.FNAME	A.LNAME	A.STATE	B.FNAME	B.LNAME
Mark	Feldman	AZ	Mary	DeMott
Lance	Roberts	AZ	Mary	DeMott
Lance	Roberts	AZ	Mark	Feldman
Mary	Bennett	FL	Elizabeth	Floyd
Connie	DeMarco	IL	Jonathan	Drake
Martha	Redwood	KY	David	Braverman

Figure 5.3   Finding people who live in the same state.
(Joining a table to itself using alias names.)

Aliases may be used in long select statements to make the meaning clearer, to assign to tables names which more closely reflect their use in the particular select statement. Aliases may also be used to avoid ambiguity.

Joining a Table to Itself

Alias names may be used to treat a single table as though it were multiple tables and to match records within that table using join columns, just as we have done previously with separate tables. We could find those persons in our PEOPLE table who have the same profession with the following statement:

```
SELECT A.FNAME, A.LNAME, A.PROF, B.FNAME, B.LNAME FROM
PEOPLE A, PEOPLE B WHERE (A.PROF = B.PROF) AND
(A.ID > B.ID);
```

We gave the PEOPLE table two aliases, 'A' and 'B', and then selected records as though we were selecting from two distinct tables. The condition 'A.ID > B.ID' was necessary in order to eliminate duplicate selections. Without the 'ID' condition, SQL would have given us each match twice:

Margaret	Langer	Doctor	Mark	Feldman
Mark	Feldman	Doctor	Margaret	Langer

It would even have matched each person with themselves. The 'ID' condition ensures that no record will be matched with itself and that each match will be selected only once.

A.FNAME	A.LNAME	A.STATE	B.FNAME	B.LNAME
Mark	Feldman	AZ	Mary	DeMott
Lance	Roberts	AZ	Mary	DeMott
Lance	Roberts	AZ	Mark	Feldman
Mary	Bennett	FL	Elizabeth	Floyd
Connie	DeMarco	IL	Jonathan	Drake
Martha	Redwood	KY	David	Braverman
Jennifer	Mallory	NY		
Margaret	Langer	CA		
Daisy	Escher	MI		
David	Dryden	CO		

Figure 5.4   The OUTER JOIN of people who live in the same state.

DesignNote: In designing systems of tables, you must be on the look-out for data which lends itself to being used in join columns. Lacking natural ways of joining tables, you may have to create fields specifically for that purpose, and must consider creating a join column if only for use in selecting records from within a single table. The ID field in the PEOPLE table, providing a *unique* identifier for each record, allows us to do things which we would not be able to do without it.

5.5   The Outer Join

Every join, in a way, creates two tables: the table which is composed of those records that meet the join conditions, and a table composed of those records which *do not* meet the join conditions. SQL, of course, will only display to the user one of these tables, the one whose records meet the conditions stated in the select statement. But it might very well be of some interest to see the records which do not join, the records from table 'A' whose join columns find no match in table 'B'. It might be valuable to see a listing, as in Figure 5.4, of those records which do join, followed by those records which do not join. Such a listing, such a table, is called an OUTER JOIN. It is a table which joins records meeting the join conditions as well as records which fall *outside* the conditions.

How can we create an outer join using SQL? Well, in standard SQL we can't. There is *no support* in the ANSI standard for an outer join operation. There are elaborate and awkward ways to patch together an outer join, which, depending upon how closely your implementation follows the standard, may or may not work. Some vendors have provided an outer join operator with their implementations of SQL, but these are peculiar to each product.

The outer join, even if it is unavailable to us, is a valuable concept, for recognizing and understanding it will further your understanding of SQL and how it manipulates tables of data.

6. Queries Within Queries

Patience wears out stones.

SELECT ASSISTANT FROM PERSONNEL
WHERE APPROACH = 'PERSISTENT';

6.1 Fluency

The language is nearly ours now. We have come into a foreign land of potentially great expanse, and we have learned most of the elements of the language spoken there. We have learned its parts and where they may be placed in constructing sentences. But we are not yet poets, or orators, or teachers. We can as yet form only simple sentences, ones that plod from subject to verb to modifying clause. Although we can form short sentences and sentences of great length, they all resemble one another, with parts included or left out. We cannot place clauses within clauses, sentences within sentences. We cannot yet build sentences which enclose, and are fed by, other sentences. The ability to do such things will imbue us with SQL fluency, and allow us to say anything that may be said with the language.

The ability to *do* anything that may be done with the language requires far more than fluency. We are all fluent in English, but few of us are poets. With every new advance in your SQL proficiency you must again regard the relational architecture and its major structures, the tables; you must again wonder what may be done with such tools, what subtleties may be wrung from them, and *how* these things can be expressed in SQL. Every advance in the power of expression is potentially an advance in the depth of perception, and to perceive structures more deeply is often to see how they might be improved and rebuilt.

As with any language, the value of proficiency lies not in the glib use of the language itself, but in what may be learned through the use of the language. It is an exploratory instrument and should be used to *change* its subject matter as well as for description.

6.2   The Subquery

All equations have a left side and a right side. Any object or term which may appear on the left side is a left-side term and any which may appear on the right side is a right-side term. In the equation below 'A' is a left-side term and 'B' is a right-side term:

$$A = B$$

In the language of mathematics, you can manipulate equations so that anything which appears on the right side may be made to appear on the left side. In computer languages this is not true; there are often terms and expressions which may appear *only* on the left side or *only* on the right. We have seen many equation-like constructions in SQL, within the WHERE clause:

$$\text{select} \ldots \text{where A} = \text{B};$$
$$\text{select} \ldots \text{where A} < \text{B};$$
$$\text{select} \ldots \text{where A} >= \text{B};$$

A SUBQUERY is a full select statement used as the right-side expression within a where clause. It is "sub-" in that it is a query which is subordinate to, or inside of, another query:

$$\text{select A} \ldots \text{where B} = (\text{select C from} \ldots);$$

A subquery should always be written within parentheses to make the full query more readable.

A subquery "feeds" the left-side term of a where clause. It reaches out to another table, or a number of tables, evaluates rows and columns, and returns values which are given to the left side of the where clause, and which are in turn evaluated within the context of the enclosing select statement. We could list the full name of every city represented in our PEOPLE table by writing:

SELECT NAME FROM CITY WHERE ID IN
(SELECT DISTINCT CITY FROM PEOPLE);

The subquery will take from the PEOPLE table the indentifying city numbers and will present those numbers, one at a time, to the main select statement, which will use the numbers to probe the CITY table.

Numerous subqueries may be joined within a single select statement by the use of AND or OR:

```
SELECT NAME, DISTANCE, DIAMETER FROM MOONS
WHERE PLANET = (SELECT ID FROM S_SYSTEM
WHERE NAME = 'Saturn') ORDER BY DISTANCE
```

NAME	DISTANCE	DIAMETER
Mimas	186000	392
Encyladus	238000	510
Tethys	295000	1060
Dione	377000	1120
Rhea	527000	1530
Titan	1222000	5150
Hyperion	1481000	205
Iapetus	3561000	1460
Phoebe	12954000	220

Figure 6.1   The moons of Saturn.

```
SELECT FNAME, LNAME FROM PEOPLE WHERE
CITY IN (SELECT ID FROM CITY WHERE NAME = 'San Francisco')
AND STATE IN (SELECT STATE FROM STATE WHERE
NAME = 'California');
```

Here two subqueries probe two tables in order to provide values which the main select statement will use in its search.

TechNote: There is nothing in the definition of the language which limits the number of queries which may be "strung together" in a single select statement. In practice each implementaion of SQL will probably impose a maximum on the possible length of any one select statement, which will in effect determine the maximum number of subqueries that may be written.

Since a subquery is merely a select statement, subqueries may contain subqueries:

```
SELECT FNAME, LNAME FROM PEOPLE WHERE CITY IN
(SELECT ID FROM CITY WHERE STATE IN
(SELECT STATE FROM STATE WHERE NAME = 'New York'));
```

The above statement would find, in a rather roundabout fashion, anyone in our PEOPLE table from New York state.

Subqueries are powerful tools which allow a select statement, or multiple select statements, incorporating the full range of SQL syntax, to be written

```
SELECT UNIT FROM UNITS WHERE TID =
(SELECT ID FROM TABLES WHERE NAME = 'S_SYSTEM')
AND FNAME = 'DISTANCE';
```

UNIT
_____

Millions of miles from Sun

```
SELECT UNIT FROM UNITS WHERE
FNAME = 'BUDGET' AND TID =
(SELECT ID FROM TABLES WHERE NAME = 'ADVERT');
```

UNIT
_____

Dollars

Figure 6.2   Given table name and field name, find units.

---

merely to "fuel" other select statements.

Where's the Units?

Every field in a relational database has a name, the name of the column which contains the field. The field also has associated with it another name, the name of the table of which it is a part. These two names, the column name and table name, are inseparable from the field; no field can exist without them. The two names uniquely identify the column; since table names must be unique within a database and column names must be unique within a table, no other column across the entire database can match an already existing table name, column name combination. But other items of information may need to be associated with a field; the value within a field may in part be inexplicable without some additional qualification. The numbers in our MOONS table, in the DISTANCE and DIAMETER columns, would be of little use if we were unaware of what *units* they were expressed in. In a scientific database installation, there might well be hundreds of fields, expressed in many different units. In business, figures might represent dollars, pounds, deutschemarks, or yen. Our database must provide us with ways of attaching bits of information to bits of information, ways of elaborating upon, or commenting upon, items within columns.

In a relational database, information can only exist within a table. If we are to annotate the fields within our database, then we must do it through the use of tables. We have provided a means of doing this through the creation of tables named UNITS and TABLES. These tables could not have been discussed until this point in our exploration of SQL because they could not have been accessed without the subquery tool.

The TABLES table simply lists all of the tables in our system, by name, and associates a unique identification number, an id, with each. The id number will be used in other tables as a join column. These numbers are used in the UNITS table, along with field names, to attach a particualar unit to a particular numeric field. Through these connections, the units information, or potentially any other bit of information, can be selected knowing only the names of the table and field about which the information is desired (see Figure 6.2).

> *DesignNote:* Rather than assign numbers to tables, why not simply use tables names in join columns? And if we are to assign numbers to table names, why not assign numbers to column names? Well, yes, we have been inconsistent. The reason for assigning numbers, so that they may then be used as join columns, is, as we have noted earlier, that numbers require much less storage space that does text. Our inconsistency arises from the belief that an individual table name may be used much more often as a join column than any individual column name. Even in our rather small UNITS table, references to particular tables occur two and three times more frequently than references to particular columns.

6.3   Subquery Sets

If one of the comparison operators (=, <>, >, <, >=, <=) precedes a subquery, SQL will expect the subquery to return only one value. If a comparison operator is used alone and the subquery returns multiple values, SQL will deliver only an error message. In our examples, we have used the operator IN to avoid this problem (to cover ourselves just *in case* our subquery returns multiple values) but IN can only be substituted if we are testing for equality (=):

Select ... where A IN (select ...);

You can also use the negative operator NOT IN and be safe with multiple-valued subqueries, but this too will work only because the test boils down to equality.

SQL allows the use of comparison operators with multiple valued subqueries if we follow the operator with one of the words ANY, SOME, or ALL. These words, in effect, tell SQL to fetch a *set* of values within the subquery, and to "feed" some or all of the values to the main query. The word should be used between the comparison operator and the subquery:

SELECT NAME FROM MOONS WHERE DIAMETER >
ANY (SELECT (DIAMETER * 1.6) FROM S_SYSTEM);

NAME
_____

Ganymede

Titan

Moon

Io

Europa

Ganymede

Callisto

Titan

Triton

Figure 6.3   Are there moons larger than planets?

Select ... where A = ANY (select ...);
Select ... where A < ALL (select ...);

Some, Any

The operators SOME and ANY are synonymous. They may be used inter-
changeably. There is no difference in their actions. They may be used with
the equality operator (=) to function as we used the operator IN earlier
in this chapter. The following query would find the names of anyone who
lived in New York state:

SELECT FNAME, LNAME FROM PEOPLE WHERE CITY = ANY
(SELECT ID FROM CITY WHERE STATE = SOME
(SELECT STATE FROM STATE WHERE NAME = 'New York'));

We could find who had gone over budget with the following query:

SELECT FNAME, LNAME FROM PEOPLE WHERE ID = ANY
(SELECT WHO FROM ADVERT WHERE SPENT > BUDGET);

The combination, in effect, tells the subquery to form a list of each item
which meets the conditions specified in the subquery, and to then "feed"
each of those items to the main query. If you think of ANY as meaning
"each" the action may seem clearer (it is somewhat more difficult to think
of SOME as meaning "each").

```
SELECT NAME, DIAMETER FROM S_SYSTEM
WHERE (DIAMETER * 1.6) > ALL
(SELECT DIAMETER FROM MOONS);
```

NAME	DIAMETER
Sun	865400
Venus	7700
Earth	7927
Mars	4200
Jupiter	88700
Saturn	75100
Uranus	32000
Neptune	27700

Figure 6.4   Solar system objects larger than any moon.

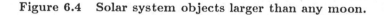

All

The operator ALL instructs the subquery to look at the values that it finds and to, in effect, return to the main query either a list of values or only a single value, depending upon which comparison operator is used. If it is used with the GREATER THAN comparison operator, it will cause the subquery to return only the largest of the values that it finds. The following query will then select names of moons that have a diameter larger than the largest of Saturn's moons:

```
SELECT NAME FROM MOONS
WHERE DIAMETER > ALL
(SELECT DIAMETER FROM MOONS
WHERE PLANET =
(SELECT ID FROM S_SYSTEM
WHERE NAME = 'Saturn'));
```

The ALL operator used in tandem with the LESS THAN comparison will return from the subquery only the least of the values selected. If ALL is used with equality (=), the subquery will return a list and the main query will select only values that match the entire list (which is possible only if all values on the list are identical). ALL used with inequality (<>) is equivalent to the syntax NOT IN.

6.4   Existence Subqueries

Subqueries may be made to test for mere existence of a certain specified condition and to return a value of "true" or "false" depending upon whether the condition was met. This may be done by using the word EXISTS to introduce the subquery. The negative term NOT EXISTS may also be used. We can find the names of everyone who has been listed against expenditures in the ADVERT table with the following query:

    SELECT FNAME, LNAME FROM PEOPLE
    WHERE EXISTS
    (SELECT * FROM ADVERT
    WHERE WHO = PEOPLE.ID);

The query instructs SQL to run through the entire PEOPLE table and, for each record, to determine if the value in the record's ID field is to be found anywhere in the WHO column of the ADVERT table, and, if so, to return a value of "true" to the main query. If the main query receives a "true" for any given record, it returns the first and last names for that record. We could find those who had *not* been listed for any expenditures by querying:

    SELECT FNAME, LNAME FROM PEOPLE
    WHERE NOT EXISTS
    (SELECT * FROM ADVERT
    WHERE WHO = PEOPLE.ID);

Here SQL will return names only from those PEOPLE records which have id values which *cannot* be found in the WHO column of the ADVERT table. We could obtain a list of the cities which were represented in the PEOPLE table with the query:

    SELECT NAME FROM CITY
    WHERE EXISTS
    (SELECT * FROM PEOPLE
    WHERE PEOPLE.CITY = CITY.ID);

Were we interested in which tables had entries in the UNITS table, we might query:

    SELECT NAME FROM TABLES
    WHERE EXISTS
    (SELECT * FROM UNITS
    WHERE TID = TABLES.ID);

TechNote: The syntax "select *" need not be used in an existence subquery. Any field or combination of fields could be selected. It simply does not matter because the subquery does not return any field values. It returns only a value of "true" or "false."

```
SELECT NAME FROM MOONS X WHERE
DIAMETER > (SELECT AVG(DIAMETER)
FROM MOONS WHERE PLANET = X.PLANET);
```

NAME

Phobos

Ganymede

Callisto

Rhea

Titan

Iapetus

Titania

Oberon

Triton

Ariel

Figure 6.5   Moons larger than average, a correlated subquery.

6.5   The Correlated Subquery

With the use of table ALIAS NAMES we can perform subqueries which are evaluated with regard to *candidate* values selected by the main query. Such queries are called CORRELATED SUBQUERIES because the subquery is executed in correlation with the candidate value of the main query.

We can use a correlated subquery to find the name of each moon in the solar system which has a diameter less than or equal to the average diameter of the moons for *that particular moon's planet*:

```
SELECT NAME FROM MOONS X WHERE
DIAMETER <= (SELECT AVG(DIAMETER)
FROM MOONS WHERE PLANET -- X.PLANET);
```

The main query will go through each record in the MOONS table and the PLANET field of each record will become a candidate value which will be "fed" to the subquery; the subquery will then find the average of all moon diameters which correlate to this candidate PLANET value, and will return that average to the main query, where it will be compared to the DIAMETER value in the candidate row. The table alias is required so that the two references to the PLANET field within the subquery may be distinguished from one another.

6.6   Union

The results of two or more queries may be "summed" with the word UNION.
The syntax involves simply placing the word between the select statements:

SELECT * from TABLEA union select * from TABLEB;

The result will be a table containing all the records selected from TABLEA
and all the records selected from TABLEB. Duplicate records will be eliminated. There are restrictions which apply to the use of UNION: the data
type and length of the fields selected from the first table must match *exactly*
the data type and length of the fields selected from the second table.

If we had stored our data on solar system moons in separate tables for
each planet instead of in a single table, we could gather the moons of Jupiter
and those of Saturn together with the following query:

    SELECT NAME, DISTANCE, DIAMETER FROM JUPITER
    UNION
    SELECT NAME, DISTANCE, DIAMETER FROM SATURN;

If more than two queries are to be "added," the unions must be parenthe-
sized:

    SELECT NAME, DISTANCE, DIAMETER FROM JUPITER
    UNION
    (SELECT NAME, DISTANCE, DIAMETER FROM SATURN
    UNION
    SELECT NAME, DISTANCE, DIAMETER FROM NEPTUNE);

7. The View

*The foolish and the dead alone
never change their opinions.*

CREATE VIEW TODAY AS SELECT
CONFIRMED, PROBABLE FROM
YESTERDAY, TOMORROW;

7.1   Seeing Anew

It is the gift of the artist and the scientist alike to be able to take the disparate, strip the dissimilarities, and recognize the connected whole which no other had seen. It is the gift of the officer and the manager alike to be able to build disparate parts which will, one day, when needed, meld and mesh and work as one. It is the job of the database designer and administrator to do all of these things with the tools at hand, the tables. Parts must be built that will combine to make larger parts, which in turn will combine. The connecting threads must be there from the beginning. Reconnections must be recognized. The users' visions must be realized. In short, the builder must populate her database with parts that are nimble and "fast on their feet," and, having done so, she must have the vision, day to day, to see where those parts might dart to to get this done, and scramble to to get that done.

The facility within SQL which allows the builder to fragment and regather tables is the VIEW. A view is, as its name implies, simply a particular "look" at the database, a framed scene which includes certain selected parts of the whole. A view, like everything else in the relational architecture, is a TABLE, and the frame, which defines and holds the view, is a select statement.

Base and Virtual Tables

Although a view is a table, it does not exist within the database as a table. It is not allocated storage space and assigned data. Tables which *do* really exist, which do occupy storage, which are brought into existence with the CREATE TABLE command, are called BASE tables. You should think of "base" as in "basic" or fundamental, for without tables there can be no database, and the base tables are *the* tables. A view, on the other hand, is called a VIRTUAL table. "Virtual" is computer jargon for anything which has a logical, or perceptual, existence, but no physical existence. The creation of a view defines a table, but only the definition is recorded and stored; the table itself, although you may query it just as any other table, has no physical existence and occupies no space within the database.

7.2   Creating Views

A view may be created with the words CREATE VIEW. The view must be given a name, and the name must not conflict with any table name which already exists:

create view MYVIEW ... ;

The contents and structure of a view are defined by writing a select statement. The select statement, in effect, *is* the view, and the CREATE VIEW syntax defines the view *as* the select statement, using the word AS:

create view MYVIEW as select ... ;

The field names within a view may be specified or they may be copied from those fields specified in the select statement, if there is no conflict (if more than a single table appears in the select statement, they may contain fields with identical names). If field names are to be specified, they are done so following the view name, as a list, separated by commas, and enclosed within parentheses:

create view MYVIEW (MYFIELDA, MYFIELDB) as select ... ;

If one of our database users simply could not abide the table name MOONS and insisted that it be named "satellites," we might satisfy him by creating a view which was identical to the MOONS table:

CREATE VIEW SATELLITES AS SELECT * FROM MOONS;

If he, furthermore, objected to our field names, we might incorporate names of his choice in our view:

CREATE VIEW SATELLITES (P, N, DIS, DIA) AS
SELECT PLANET, NAME, DISTANCE, DIAMETER FROM MOONS;

Once created, the view may be queried with all the tools which have developed for probing tables:

SELECT N, DIS, DIA FROM SATELLITES WHERE P =
(SELECT ID FROM S_SYSTEM WHERE NAME = 'Jupiter');

The above query would retrieve information about Jupiter's moons just as would a select performed upon the base table MOONS.

The flexibility provided by the view goes beyond selecting from base tables. The query defining a view may select from a view or from a number of views, or it may select from a combination of base tables and views. Having framed portions of base tables and "sighted" that data through the creation of views, you may then frame selected portions of those views and sight into those portions with yet more views. The virtual tables may comprise bits of other virtual tables.

> *TechNote:* Flexibility comes at a cost. Views do, of course, occupy *some* space within the database, the space needed to store the view definition, the select statement specified in the CREATE VIEW statement. The real piece that must be paid for views, however, is *time.* When a select statement is performed on a view, the database "engine" must first retrieve the view definition, find which base tables are named there, and which fields within those tables are being selected. It must then compose a "real" select statement, one which references base tables. Only after it has translated all virtual names into names of existing database items may it begin to retrieve data. Translation always takes time. Depending upon the complexity of the views being queried, and upon the power of your SQL implementation, you may notice some difference in the speed with which data is retrieved from views compared with the speed when base tables are referenced directly.

7.3   Tables Within Tables

A view may be used to create one table from a portion of another table. Our use of the database may require that we consult certain fields of a table far more often than other fields. Or it may be that we often consult one group of fields, and, just as often, consult a different group from the same table. Simply for the sake of convenience, and to save the necessity of repeatedly typing long and convoluted select statements, these situations would call for the creation of views. Views can be restricted to certain fields in the underlying table, by specifically naming only those fields in the CREATE VIEW statement. Restrictions may be placed upon the range of records which a view may return, by using a WHERE clause within the view definition.

```
CREATE VIEW SPENT
(FIRST, LAST, WHEN, SPENT) AS
SELECT FNAME, LNAME, WHEN, SPENT
FROM PEOPLE, ADVERT
WHERE ID = WHO;

SELECT * FROM SPENT;
```

FIRST	LAST	WHEN	SPENT
Jennifer	Mallory	31-DEC-86	212.34
David	Dryden	05-JAN-87	327.65
Lance	Roberts	15-JAN-87	443.09
Elizabeth	Floyd	21-JAN-87	106.73
Mary	DeMott	29-JAN-87	52.88

Figure 7.1   Who spent what, and when.

If we wanted to regularly review what had been budgeted for the advertising department, without regard to what had or had not actually been spent, we might create a view of the ADVERT table:

```
CREATE VIEW BUDGET AS
SELECT WHEN, WHAT, BUDGET FROM ADVERT
WHERE BUDGET NOT NULL;
```

Since we will use this view to look at what amounts *have* been budgeted, we have excluded from the view items for which no budget was set.

We can use views to do arithmetic for us, creating new fields from manipulations of existing data (see Figure 7.3). Permanent access to pre-tax cost of items in the ADVERT table might be provided through a view:

```
CREATE VIEW SPENT
(WHEN, WHAT, PRETAX, TAX) AS
SELECT WHEN, WHAT,
(SPENT − TAX), TAX
FROM ADVERT;
```

Here we had to specify field names for the view because the field created by taking the difference between SPENT and TAX did not exist in the base table.

If one of our astronomers specialized in the "outer planets," we might spare her from having to see data on the inner planets' moons:

```
CREATE VIEW OUTER AS
SELECT NAME, DISTANCE, DIAMETER
FROM MOONS WHERE PLANET = ANY
(SELECT ID FROM S_SYSTEM WHERE DISTANCE >
(SELECT DISTANCE FROM S_SYSTEM WHERE
NAME = 'Mars'));
```

The select statement which serves to define the view being created may be of any complexity, and may contain nested subqueries to whatever level your particular SQL implementation will allow.

Security

Views may be created as imaginative ways of rearranging existing data, or they may be created merely for the sake of convenience. They can also serve as security devices, to hide and protect sensitive data. A user may select from a view only those fields and records which are included in the underlying definition. If, within that definition, a WHERE clause excludes a certain range of records, then there is no way in which a user can access those records through that view. To take a rather fanciful instance, if dissemination of data concerning Jupiter's moons were suddenly deemed a security risk, we might restrict user access to planetary satellite data through the following view:

```
CREATE VIEW SATELLITE AS
SELECT * FROM MOONS
WHERE PLANET <>
(SELECT ID FROM S_SYSTEM
WHERE NAME = 'Jupiter');
```

Our security would be of little value if users had access to the base tables from which the views were derived. To provide a more thorough security we would have to combine views with the granting of privileges, which are discussed in a later chapter.

7.4   Tables Among Tables

Views may be created by selecting bits and pieces from various tables, or from other views, and combining them to form what will appear to be a single, seamless table (see Figures 7.1 and 7.2). We might bring together full state names with full city names in the following view:

```
CREATE VIEW CITY_STATE
(CNAME, SABBR, SNAME) AS
SELECT CITY.NAME, CITY.STATE, STATE.NAME
FROM CITY, STATE WHERE
CITY.STATE = STATE.STATE;
```

```
CREATE VIEW HOME
(FNAME, LNAME, CITY, STATE) AS
SELECT FNAME, LNAME,
CITY.NAME, STATE.NAME FROM
PEOPLE, CITY, STATE WHERE
(PEOPLE.CITY = CITY.ID) AND
(PEOPLE.STATE = STATE.STATE);

SELECT * FROM HOME;
```

FNAME	LNAME	CITY	STATE
Mary	DeMott	Flagstaff	Arizona
Mark	Feldman	Flagstaff	Arizona
Lance	Roberts	Flagstaff	Arizona
Margaret	Langer	San Francisco	California
David	Dryden	Denver	Colorado
Elizabeth	Floyd	Miami	Florida
Mary	Bennett	Miami	Florida
Jonathan	Drake	Chicago	Illinois
Connie	DeMarco	Chicago	Illinois
David	Braverman	Lexington	Kentucky
Martha	Redwood	Lexington	Kentucky
Daisy	Escher	Lansing	Michigan
Jennifer	Mallory	New York	New York

Figure 7.2   Viewing three tables: who lives where.

We could then take a piece of the above view and combine it with a bit of the PEOPLE table to form a full list of people's names with their respective city and state all nicely written out, and with no abbreviations:

```
CREATE VIEW NAME_PLACE
(FNAME, LNAME, CITY, STATE) AS
SELECT FNAME, LNAME, CNAME, SNAME
FROM PEOPLE, CITY_STATE WHERE
STATE = SABBR;
```

The creation of this view does not require that full field names be specified, since all field names are unique across the table and the view which underlay the new database object.

```
CREATE VIEW MP (P, PD, M, MD) AS
SELECT S_SYSTEM.NAME, S_SYSTEM.DIAMETER,
MOONS.NAME, (MOONS.DIAMETER / 1.6) FROM
S_SYSTEM, MOONS WHERE ID = PLANET;

SELECT P, PD, M, MD, (MD/PD)
FROM MP ORDER BY (MD/PD) DESC;
```

P	PD	M	MD	(MD/PD)
Pluto	1500	Charon	750	.5000
Earth	7927	Moon	2175	.2743
Neptune	27700	Triton	2500	.0902
Saturn	75100	Titan	3218	.0428
Jupiter	88700	Ganymede	3297	.0371
Jupiter	88700	Callisto	3012	.0339
Uranus	32000	Oberon	1012	.0316
Uranus	32000	Titania	1000	.0312
Jupiter	88700	Io	2270	.0255
Uranus	32000	Ariel	812	.0253
Jupiter	88700	Europa	1953	.0220
Uranus	32000	Umbriel	687	.0214
Saturn	75100	Rhea	956	.0127
Saturn	75100	Iapetus	912	.0121
Neptune	27700	Neried	312	.0112
Saturn	75100	Dione	700	.0093
Saturn	75100	Tethys	662	.0088
Uranus	32000	Miranda	200	.0062
Saturn	75100	Encyladus	318	.0042
Mars	4200	Phobos	16	.0040
Saturn	75100	Mimas	245	.0032
Mars	4200	Deimos	9	.0022
Saturn	75100	Phoebe	137	.0018
Saturn	75100	Hyperion	128	.0017

Figure 7.3   A VIEW of planet/moon size ratios, in miles.

Merely from the simple samples above, the power and flexibility of the view can readily be seen. Without entering into the database a single item of data, without even moving any data, we can create fully populated tables. Since views are brought into the world at very nearly no cost, we can experiment and play, picturing these bits of data today, and framing those bits tomorrow, all the while seeing the old familiar data anew, finding new relationships, and, perhaps, creating views that will abide and be used by every user every day.

7.5 Deleting Views

Views may be removed from the database with the simple words DROP VIEW. The words are followed by the name of the view to be destroyed:

    DROP VIEW MYVIEW;

Since views are "virtual," and contain no data in themselves, SQL simply removes the view definition from its storage place. No data need be deleted.

8. Changing Records

Use soft words and hard arguments.

UPDATE OPPONENTS SET THOUGHTS =
(SELECT WISDOM FROM EXPERIENCE);

8.1   Righting Wrongs

Nothing is more certain than the creeping in of errors when a sentient creature is sentenced to hour upon hour of data entry. Mistakes will be made. Corrections will be mandated.

Many databases are filled by "downloading" data from other databases; information from academic or governmental sources is thus made available for local use and for further dissemination. Such information is rarely error-free. The sources will periodically post corrections of past errors, or incorrect data may be discovered locally. Changes will have to be made.

Users will object to the ways in which data is presented. The business community might object to distances expressed in kilometers, whereas the scientific community might insist upon such expression. No matter what the expression, *someone* will object, and, should that someone become legion, the decision will be taken to alter fields, perhaps many, many fields.

Change will always find a home in any large and complex ordering. Databases which are active, which are useful and *used*, have little truck with the immutable. SQL's facility for changing that which it has created is as subtle and as varied as its ability to query what it has stored.

71

8.2   Update

The SQL verb which effects change is UPDATE. It is always accompanied by the verb SET. The two verbs will bracket the name of the table which is to be changed:

update MYTABLE set ... ;

The specific action which is to be taken is expressed by a field name, an equal sign, and a value which is to be placed into the field:

update MYTABLE set MYFIELD = 'xyz' ... ;

Numerous actions may be specified by using the comma as a separator:

update MYTABLE set FLDA = 1, FLDB = 2 ... ;

Changes may be restricted to a specific record or to a group of records through the use of a WHERE clause:

update MYTABLE set FLDA = 12.34 where ... ;

If no WHERE clause is included, SQL will make the specified change in *every* record of the table. The inclusion of a WHERE clause instructs SQL to go to the table, locate the records which meet the conditions specified in the WHERE clause, and effect the specified changes only upon those records.

A useful verb, UPDATE. And, potentially, a very dangerous one. If, at data entry, Patty Periwinkle's name had been misspelled, and we set about correcting it with the following statement:

UPDATE PEOPLE SET LNAME = 'Periwinkle';

Well, we would then have to set about correcting everyone else's name, for the above statement would set *all* last names to 'Periwinkle.' A more certain procedure would be to write:

UPDATE PEOPLE SET LNAME = 'Periwinkle'
WHERE (LNAME = 'Pariwinkle') AND
(FNAME = 'Patricia');

Even this statement is not absolutely safe, for if there were a person whose real name was *Patricia Pariwinkle,* we would have incorrectly altered her name; we would have introduced into the database one mistake while correcting another. Care must be taken that the WHERE clause in an UPDATE statement will select those and *only* those records which need changing. If there is any uncertainty as to which records will be changed, a SELECT statement using the same WHERE clause will display the records which would be processed by the UPDATE statement.

DesignNote: Imagine a table containing thousands upon thousands of records, and imagine that you need to alter one record, only one particular record. How do you specify one and only one record with complete certainty? Well, you may not be able to, unless you have foreseen this eventuality and designed uniqueness into your table. If all records differ from one another in at least one field, then you can

```
UPDATE MOONS SET
DISTANCE = DISTANCE / 1.6,
DIAMETER = DIAMETER / 1.6;

UPDATE UNITS SET
UNIT = 'Miles'
WHERE (FNAME = 'DIAMETER')
AND (TID _ (SELECT ID FROM
TABLES WHERE NAME = 'MOONS'));

UPDATE UNITS SET
UNIT = 'Miles from planet'
WHERE (FNAME = 'DISTANCE')
AND (TID = (SELECT ID FROM
TABLES WHERE NAME = 'MOONS'));
```

Figure 8.1   Changing kilometers to miles.

---

always specify a record uniquely, even if you have to designate *every* field in the WHERE clause. This *should* always be the case, with *all* tables. Tables should be designed so as to *disallow* records which are exact duplicates of one another. In the relational architecture, records are *not ordered*, and therefore records which are identical in every field are *indistinguishable*. To enter into a table records which are identical in every field is to store the same bit of information multiple times, and this is senseless. The uniqueness of records can be mandated through the creation of a unique INDEX (see the discussion of indexes in the chapter on *Table Creation*), and may be implemented through the use of fields containing arbitrary, unique numbers, such as the ID field in some of our tables.

We could change the SPENT column in the ADVERT table to reflect pre-tax cost rather than total cost with the following statement:

UPDATE ADVERT SET SPENT = (SPENT − TAX);

Of course, we could only execute the above statement once, and thereafter would have to enter pre-tax cost into the SPENT column. We could change Jennifer Mallory's profession with the following statement:

UPDATE PEOPLE SET PROF = 'Judge'
WHERE FNAME = 'Jennifer' AND LNAME = 'Mallory'
AND PROF = 'Lawyer';

Data Types

The new values which are to be placed into fields must conform to the data type for that field. Only numeric values, whether positive or negative, may be placed into numeric fields:

> ...set NUMBERFIELD = 12.37...;
>
> ...set NUMBERFIELD = −35...;

Character strings may be placed only into character fields. The strings must be enclosed in single quotation marks, and the string must not exceed the maximum length of the field into which it is being placed:

> ...set TEXTFIELD = '123 Maple Drive'...;
>
> ...set TEXTFIELD = 'Jennifer'...;

When a field is to be set equal to some other field, then the two fields must be of the same data type.

Null

If it were suddenly announced that all measurements for the moons of Uranus were incorrect and would have to be recalculated after further exploration, we might decide to set our table values to "unknown" while we awaited the new values:

```
UPDATE MOONS SET
DISTANCE = NULL,
DIAMETER = NULL
WHERE PLANET =
SELECT ID FROM S_SYSTEM WHERE
NAME = 'Uranus';
```

It should be noted that the syntax here is different from that required when using nulls in a WHERE clause. In a WHERE clause we are required to use the syntax IS NULL or IS NOT NULL, rather than using a null in conjunction with an equal sign:

> ...where MYFIELD is null...;
>
> ...where MYFIELD is not null...;

This is one of a number of instances where the SQL language definition strays into inconsistencies, allowing a particular syntax in one construction, while barring it from another.

9. Record Creation and Deletion

Sweet is the memory of past labor.

INSERT INTO TOMORROW (JOB1, JOB2)
VALUES ('COMPLETED', 'COMPLETED');

9.1 Data Entry

A surprising number of those who first venture upon the road of imple-
menting a computerized store of information have very little notion of how
their bits and peices, having been gathered, will enter into the computer.
They rarely have in mind one person, or a staff of people, sitting for hour
upon hour, hands at keyboards and eyes darting back and forth from paper
to screen. It is a task which, despite its tedium, requires alertness and care.
It is a task which can never keep up with the information which the world
can produce. One industrious individual can easily gather enough material
to keep a data entry staff occupied full time.

Neither the query's finesse and finery nor the report's geometrical order
can come into being until the database has been populated. The data entry
people and the sentences which they use are the unsung Sherpas who haul
mountains of gear to the mountain and thus allow the glamorous climbers
their triumphs. Familiarity with the ways in which records are added to the
database and expertise in streamlining these processes are vitally important
to anyone who would build or manage a computerized information fount.

9.2   Insert

The SQL verb which creates new records is INSERT. It is always accompanied by the word INTO, which is directly followed by the name of the table to which the new record is to be added:

insert into MYTABLE . . . ;

The data which is to be added is introduced by the word VALUES and is enclosed in parentheses, with data items separated by commas:

insert into MYTABLE values (1, 'Mary', 23.5, 'Periwinkle');

All fields in the new record may be filled with data or a reocrd may be created with only some of its fields filled. If only certain fields are to be filled, the names of those fields are specified immediately following the table name, enclosed in parentheses, and separated by commas:

insert into MYTABLE (FIELDA, FIELDB) . . . ;

Fields which are not named, which are not assigned some bit of data, will be given a null value.

We could create a new record in the MOONS table, filling all fields, with the following statement:

INSERT INTO MOONS VALUES (5, 'Io', 422000, 3632);

Or we could leave the join column to be filled in later, adding the new record with only three of its fields given values:

INSERT INTO MOONS (NAME, DISTANCE, DIAMETER)
VALUES ('Io', 422000, 3632);

We could specifically set the join column to a null value with the following statement:

INSERT INTO MOONS VALUES (NULL, 'Io', 422000, 3632);

Fields need not be filled in the order in which they were defined when the table was created. We may specify the fields to be filled in whatever order we wish:

INSERT INTO MOONS (DIAMETER, DISTANCE, NAME)
VALUES (3632, 422000, 'Io');

Whenever a new record is added to the database, the *data type* of each new data item must correspond to the data type of the field into which it is being placed. If a new record is created without specifying data items for some of its fields, then those fields will be set to null *only if*, at table creation, those fields were defined as accepting null values. If, at table creation, a field were designated as NOT NULL, then a data value would have to be specified for that field whenever a new record were added to the database.

Inserting With Subqueries

Rather than using a VALUES clause to specify data items to be inserted into a new record, we may create new records in one table by gathering data items from other tables, through the use of a subquery. The subquery simply replaces the VALUES clause in the INSERT statement:

insert into MYTABLE select ... ;

Again, particular fields may be specified:

insert into MYTABLE (FIELDA, FIELDB) select ... ;

The subquery may be any valid select statement, with one restriction—it may *not* reference the table into which the new records are being inserted. The following syntax is disallowed in the ANSI standard:

insert into MYTABLE select * from MYTABLE;

The statement is illegal because the data to be used in the creation of new records is being taken from the same table in which the new records are being created. The same statement would be perfectly correct if the data were selected from a second table:

insert into MYTABLE select * from YOURTABLE;

Data type restrictions, of course, apply when subqueries are used, just as they do in the use of the VALUES clause. The data which is selected for inclusion in the newly created records must be of the same type as that which the new records were defined to accept.

Whereas use of the VALUES clause creates just one new record for each insert statement which is executed, using the subquery will, usually, result in the creation of a number of new records. One new record will be created in the target table for each record which is returned by the select statement.

If we, for whatever reason, created a table which would hold nothing but the names of the people in our PEOPLE table, we could fill the new table with the following statement:

INSERT INTO JUST_NAMES (FNAME, LNAME)
SELECT FNAME, LNAME FROM PEOPLE;

If we wanted to restrict our new table to the medical profession, we could write:

INSERT INTO JUST_NAMES (FNAME, LNAME)
SELECT FNAME, LNAME FROM PEOPLE
WHERE PROF = 'Doctor';

DesignNote: Those who are responsible for maintaining a database are often expected to find more efficient ways of doing whatever it is the database is intended to do, as well to find efficient ways to do new things. Because of the peculiarities of various hardware configurations, and the varying strengths and weaknesses of different database implementations, it is often not possible to predict the one alternative out of many which will get the chore done fastest. One must simply experiment. In order to do this, one must have objects, namely tables, upon which to experiment. Sometimes one needs to play with *large* tables. The question is, how does one quickly create a large table to experiment with? Well, if you don't mind having duplicate records in your experimental table, you can very quickly build a test table of any size by simply selecting into that table all of the records from another table; and then do it again, and again... You perform an INSERT with a "select *" subquery, which will copy all the records from the selected table into the test table. You then perform the same statement again, which will *again* copy all the records to the test table. Each time the statement is executed, the test table will be incremented in size by the full size of the selected table. Soon you will have a very large table to play with.

Subqueries within an INSERT statement may be of any complexity. We could bring the moons of Jupiter into a table of their own with the following statement:

```
INSERT INTO J_MOONS (NAME, DISTANCE, DIAMETER)
SELECT NAME, DISTANCE, DIAMETER FROM MOONS
WHERE PLANET = (SELECT ID FROM S_SYSTEM
WHERE NAME = 'Jupiter');
```

The subquery could also gather fields from a number of tables, to be ordered into new records in a new table.

9.3   Beyond The Standard

Having to type in the data values for hundreds or even thousands of records is no mean task, but if the data entry staff were also required to retype, over and over, these rather long and cumbersome INSERT statements, well, they might decide to seek some new line of work. Although the ANSI standard makes no mention of such utilities, some commercial database implementations provide ways of easily re-executing an insert statement. You may be able to type "run", or simply "r", in order to have the statement execute again. This, however, does not entirely solve your problem; if you simply re-execute the same statement, the same data values will be entered into each new record. Some implementations allow you to place special characters in the VALUES clause, which, when executed, will cause the computer to prompt the user for the data:

```
INSERT INTO MOONS (DIAMETER, DISTANCE, NAME)
VALUES (??, ??, ??);
```

If a double question mark were the special characters, the above statement could be run repeatedly, and each time it would prompt the user to enter

```
INSERT INTO ADVERT (WHEN, WHAT, SPENT, TAX)
VALUES ('21-JAN 87', 'Dinner for 4', 106.73, 6.40);


INSERT INTO CITY VALUES (13, 'Lansing', 'MI');


INSERT INTO DUMMY VALUES (0);


INSERT INTO MOONS (NAME, DISTANCE, DIAMETER)
VALUES ('Miranda', 130000, 320);


INSERT INTO PEOPLE (FNAME, LNAME, PROF) VALUES
('Martha', 'Redwood', 'Accountant');


INSERT INTO S_SYSTEM VALUES
(4, 'Mars', 141, 4200);


INSERT INTO STATE VALUES ('Idaho', 'ID');


INSERT INTO TABLES VALUES (5, 'Units');


INSERT INTO UNITS (FNAME, UNIT)
VALUES ('DISTANCE', 'Kilometers from planet');
```

Figure 9.1   Populating our tables.

values for the three fields. The insert statement itself would not need to be retyped.

9.4   Deleting Records

Records may be removed from tables with the verb DELETE. It is always followed by the word FROM which is in turn followed by. the name of the table from which the records are to be removed:

> delete from MYTABLE ... ;

Specific records are chosed for deletion through the addition of a WHERE clause. If no WHERE clause is specified, then *all* records will be removed from the named table:

    DELETE FROM PEOPLE;

The above statement would leave the PEOPLE table empty. We could select a particular record for deletion with the following statement:

    DELETE FROM PEOPLE WHERE
    FNAME = 'David' AND LNAME = 'Dryden';

The WHERE clause may contain a SELECT statement of any complexity. We could remove the moons of the two giant planets from our table by writing:

    DELETE FROM MOONS WHERE PLANET IN
    (SELECT ID FROM S_SYSTEM WHERE
    (NAME = 'Jupiter') OR
    (NAME = 'Saturn'));

10. Table Creation and Deletion

All glory comes from daring to begin.

CREATE TABLE TABLE1
(FIELD1 NUMBER);

10.1 The Ease of the Thing

One of the genuine pleasures of the relational model is the facility with which new objects may be created and old objects may be discarded; and, combining creation and destruction, the ease with which objects may be molded and transformed. The objects are the carriers of information, the stores—tables. Unless you yourself have had to do it, you will not easily credit the amount of work that can be involved in making even the most minute of changes to the structure of databases which have been cast in certain architectures other than relational. There are database implementations which require that, before a database may be created, every record type and its structure must be declared, and that, once a database is created, no record structure may be changed, nor may new record structures be added. To accede to a user's need for new record structures, a database administrator (it would, in fact, probably require someone even more immersed in the technical morass, a systems programmer, or such) would have to create an entirely new, empty database, containing all the record structures of the old, and, in addition, the new record structures. All of the data in the old database must then be moved to the new database, with the movement perhaps requiring some custom programming. The old

81

database would then be destroyed, and all application programs pointed at the new database (after they were changed to accommodate the new structures). All of this assumes that the site contains enough storage space to hold two entire databases; without that the change is simply impossible. A good deal of work indeed, and, once done, it suffices only until another user comes up with another needed record structure.

10.2   Creating Tables

In the relational architecture, the creation of a table requires only that a table name be chosen, that at least one field, and its name, be assigned to that table, and that the data *type* of the field be specified. The verb is CREATE and we must specify that we are creating a TABLE:

                    create table . . . ;

The name of the table follows immediately after the word TABLE. Any name may be chosen, so long as a table of that name does not already exist, and providing that the name is not one of SQL's reserved words (see Appendix B):

                    create table MYTABLE . . . ;

A table cannot exist unless it contains at least one field, and every field must be named. The field name may not be one of SQL's reserved words, and it must be unique only *within the table*. Field names may be duplicated many times across an entire database, but must be unique within a single table. The field name follows the table name and must be placed within parentheses:

                create table MYTABLE (MYFIELD . . .);

The field name, of course, also specifies the name of the column of which the field will be a member. No field may be created without specifiying a data type for that field (see the discussion of field types in Chapter 1). The field type is specified immediately following the field name:

            create table MYTABLE (MYFIELD NUMBER . . .);

A field length may be specified, and with some field types, *must* be specified. The length is specified, in parentheses, immediately following the field type:

            create table MYTABLE (MYFIELD NUMBER(5) . . .);

The above bits and pieces would come together in the following SQL statement:

    CREATE TABLE MYTABLE (MYFIELD NUMBER(5));

Multiple fields are created simply by separating the field specifications by a comma:

    CREATE TABLE MYTABLE
    (FIELD1 CHAR(20), MYFIELD NUMBER(5));

```
CREATE TABLE ADVERT
(WHO NUMBER NOT NULL, WHEN DATE NOT NULL,
WHAT CHAR(40) NOT NULL, BUDGET NUMBER,
SPENT NUMBER NOT NULL, TAX NUMBER);

CREATE TABLE MOONS
(PLANET NUMBER NOT NULL UNIQUE, NAME CHAR(30),
DISTANCE NUMBER, DIAMETER NUMBER);

CREATE TABLE STATE
(NAME CHAR(40), STATE CHAR(2) NOT NULL UNIQUE);
```

Figure 10.1   Creating tables.

The number of fields that may be created within a single table will be limited by the particular implementation which you are using. The ANSI standard does not specify a maximum number of fields per table.

With a few wrinkles to be discussed below, that is pretty much it for creating tables. With the statement above, a table called MYTABLE would exist in the database. Rows and columns of data could be added to it and all of the select statements which we have discussed could be exercised upon it. We could just as easily create MYTABLE2, MYTABLE3, and so on...

TechNote: Although a "SELECT *" statement will most likely present a table's fields in the order in which they were created, fields in the relational architecture are not considered as *ordered*. Fields within a record are *related*, just as are records within a table. No order is implied, either among fields within the record or among records within the table.

Not Null

When a field is defined it may be specified that it *must* contain data, that it may not be a null field. The words which specify this restriction are NOT NULL and they follow immediately after the field type:

```
CREATE TABLE MYTABLE
(FIELD1 CHAR(20) NOT NULL, MYFIELD NUMBER(5));
```

The above statement creates a table, MYTABLE, containing one field, FIELD1, which SQL will not allow to exist unless it contains data. If an attempt is made to create a record specifying a null value for the field FIELD1, SQL will reject the attempt and deliver an error message.

In Figure 10.1 we specified that, in the ADVERT table, the WHO field is to be NOT NULL; that some person's name *must* be associated with each expenditure. We also insisted upon a date (WHEN), a description (WHAT), and an amount spent (SPENT). When we designed the table, we decided that a record could not exist unless these fields were filled in. We decided the BUDGET field *could* be null; some expenditures are not budgeted. We also allowed the TAX field to contain a null; in this case the null would mean that the tax had not yet been calculated, distinguishing it from a record which recorded no tax; which had a value of zero in the TAX field.

We specified that the PLANET field in the MOONS table and the STATE field in the STATE table both be NOT NULL. These fields are within JOIN COLUMNS and are used to uniquely identify each record so that it may be associated unambiguously with records from other tables. Since a null is equivalent to any other null, we could not allow one to exist in a field which must contain a unique value.

Unique

A field may be created as one which must contain a unique value within its column. Uniqueness may be imposed only upon fields which have been declared NOT NULL, so that SQL will allow no field to accept the UNIQUE restriction unless it has first been restricted to NOT NULL. The restriction is specified with the word UNIQUE and follows immediately after the field's data type:

```
CREATE TABLE MYTABLE
(FIELD1 CHAR(20) NOT NULL,
MYFIELD NUMBER(5) NOT NULL UNIQUE);
```

The above statement instructs SQL to accept only unique values for the field MYFIELD. Whenever a new record is added to MYTABLE, SQL will note the value being entered into MYFIELD, and will check that value against every other value in the MYFIELD column. If the new value matches an already entered value, the new record will be rejected.

Fields may be created as both NOT NULL and UNIQUE:

```
CREATE TABLE MYTABLE
(FIELD1 CHAR(20) NOT NULL UNIQUE,
MYFIELD NUMBER(5) NOT NULL UNIQUE);
```

In Figure 10.1 we specified that the JOIN COLUMNS were to be UNIQUE as well as NOT NULL. Duplicate values in such columns must be disallowed for the same reason that nulls must be—these columns are used to individually mark each record so that they may be connected to other marked records throughout the database.

DesignNote: Table structure can be changed (see Figure 10.3), but it is tiresome and tedious. It also requires that the data from the original table will be acceptable to the restructured table. If nulls or duplicate column data have been entered into a table's columns, and it is then decided to restructure the table specifying NOT NULL or UNIQUE for those same columns, it will not be possible to move the data to the redesigned table. It may require that someone go through many, many fields, changing or adding data. To avoid such situations, careful thought should be given to the nature of each field which is created. Before any data can be entered, it should be decided whether or not NOT NULL or UNIQUE should be designated.

Multiple Unique

If a table is to be created with more than a single field designated as UNIQUE, all of the UNIQUE designations may be made together at the end of the list of fields:

```
CREATE TABLE MYTABLE
(FIELD1 CHAR(20) NOT NULL,
MYFIELD NUMBER(5) NOT NULL,
UNIQUE (FIELD1, MYFIELD));
```

Note that the list of fields to operated upon by UNIQUE is enclosed in parentheses and field names are separated by commas. In the statement above the restriction UNIQUE is applied to two fields, both of which had previously been restricted to NOT NULL.

10.3   Before the Standard

Many commercial implementations of SQL, developed long before the ANSI standard, do not provide the UNIQUE operator as part of the CREATE syntax. They do not, in fact, allow uniqueness to be specified as part of a table definition. In these implementations, uniqueness may be imposed upon a field or group of fields through the creation of an INDEX. The ANSI standard departs from commercial implementations not only in the manner of enforcing uniqueness; it does not specify any syntax for creating or manipulating indexes.

TechNote: The means for enforcing uniqueness which were adopted by ANSI are not arbitrary. They do, in fact, constitute an improvement over previous practice. If uniqueness is to be imposed upon a particular column, that restriction *should* be a part of the table definition, and not something which is implemented by a mechanism external to the table itself.

Commercial implementations of SQL, such as IBM's DB2 (and, very likely, whatever one you are using), provide a CREATE INDEX statement. Every index that is created must be given a name, with the name following immediately after the CREATE INDEX. The name of the table which is to be indexed must be specified in an ON phrase following the index name. The name of the field which is to be indexed must be specified within parentheses, following the table name:

CREATE INDEX PINDEX ON PEOPLE (LNAME);

The above statement will index the LNAME field in the PEOPLE table, and will name that index PINDEX. Indexes may be created using multiple fields:

CREATE INDEX PINDEX ON PEOPLE (LNAME, FNAME);

The above statement creates an index which orders first names *within* last names.

In relational databases employing the CREATE INDEX syntax, uniqueness is enforced by specifying CREATE UNIQUE INDEX:

CREATE UNIQUE INDEX PINDEX ON PEOPLE (LNAME, FNAME);

This statement would (rather foolishly) bar people with identical first and last names from our database. Needless to say, the above statement could not be executed if the table already contained duplicate names. If uniqueness is to be properly enforced, the CREATE UNIQUE INDEX statements should be executed immediately after the CREATE TABLE statements, and before any data has been entered.

Implementations providing the CREATE INDEX syntax, of course, provide a means for deleting indexes. To remove the index created above (removing also the uniqueness restriction), we would simply write:

DROP INDEX PINDEX;

10.4   The Index

Although the ANSI committee did not specify a syntax to be used in creating indexes, any commercial SQL implementation will provide for the creation of such objects. What are these objects and how are they used?

When new records are entered into a table, SQL simply writes the new record into the space provided for that table within the database. The records are written to the table in the order in which they are entered, which is to say they are written willy-nilly. Suppose that our PEOPLE table were not as small as it is, suppose that it were a table in a government tax bureau's database. Suppose that it contained millions of records. Suppose that we had not indexed our table and that we asked SQL to find Jennifer Mallory's record. How would SQL proceed? Well, in the absence of an index, it has no choice—it would go to the table, read the first record, look at the name, and, if it were not Jennifer's record, SQL would then read the second record, and so on, potentially reading millions of records in the search for Jennifer. You might well go out to lunch and return only to find SQL still hard at work seeking Jennifer.

When we create an index we tell SQL to take all the names and rewrite them in another list, this time in alphabetical order. Furthermore, we tell SQL that, so long as the index is in existence, whenever a new name is added to the table, that name must also be added to the alphabetical list, in its proper position.

When SQL is requested to search a column which has been indexed, it goes not to the table, but to the index. There it jumps directly to the "Mallory" bit of the list, finds Jennifer's name right off, and, with other information stored in the index, is able to proceed directly to Jennifer's record in the table. SQL will have returned with the requested information before you could even *think* of going to lunch.

> *DesignNote:* In creating indexes, the database implementation must actually create an ordered copy of the data being indexed. This is not done by copying the data *itself*, but by creating *pointers* to the data. Depending upon the nature of the fields being indexed, the index could actually occupy more space within the database than the data itself. For this reason, the creation of indexes should be carefully thought out. Indexes should not be proliferated needlessly. If a table is to be indexed, thought should be given to *which* fields are to be included in the index. Fields which are short, numeric, and which are likely to be of help in a great variety of searches should be sought after.

Transparency

When a computer performs some service for a user without having to be asked, it is said that that service, that effort, is *transparent* to the user. This is meant to be a good thing. The greater the number of transparent services, the smaller the number of specific requests a user need make to get a job done.

The use of indexes by SQL should be entirely transparent to the user. Whenever a request is executed, SQL should automatically check to see if any indexes exist which might speed up the procedure. If multiple indexes exist, SQL is to decide which is preferable in light of the current request. It should never be necessary for a user to specify that an index be used or that a particular index be used. The mere existence of an index in a relational database should ensure that it will be used whenever its use would be advantageous.

ANSI DATA TYPES	
NAME	TYPE
CHARACTER	character string
CHAR	character string
NUMERIC	exact numeric
DECIMAL	exact numeric
DEC	exact numeric
INTEGER	exact numeric
INT	exact numeric
SMALLINT	exact numeric
FLOAT	approximate numeric
REAL	approximate numeric
DOUBLE PRECISION	approximate numeric

Figure 10.2   CREATE TABLE data types.

10.5   Data Types

The ANSI standard specifies only character and numeric data types for use with the CREATE TABLE statement. The data type DATE, which has been used in this book, is not specified in the standard, although many commercial databases offer it. Existing relational databases also offer data types such as TIME and MONEY. Field types such as DATE and TIME are extremely useful and will probably be added to the standard in the future. The use of the CHARACTER type in this book conforms with that defined by ANSI. A CHAR field type is declared followed by a length enclosed in parentheses:

CREATE TABLE MYTABLE (MYFIELD CHAR(5));

This statement allocates a one-character field and specifies that its maximum length is to be five characters.

This book, instead of using the numerous numeric data types defined by ANSI, has used just one numeric type declaration, NUMBER. This convention, used by some commercial implementations, allows a numeric field to be declared with no specific length (in which case the field will be assigned a default length by the database):

CREATE TABLE MYTABLE (MYFIELD NUMBER);

The above statement will assign to the field MYFIELD a numeric type with a maximum length equal to the default maximum for the particular database

```
CREATE TABLE TEMP (NEW_FIELD NUMBER, WHO NUMBER,
WHEN DATE, WHAT CHAR(40), BUDGET NUMBER,
SPENT NUMBER, TAX NUMBER);



INSERT INTO TEMP (WHO, WHEN, WHAT, BUDGET, SPENT, TAX)
SELECT WHO, WHEN, WHAT, BUDGET, SPENT, TAX
FROM ADVERT;



DELETE FROM ADVERT;



DROP TABLE ADVERT;



CREATE TABLE ADVERT (NEW_FIELD NUMBER, WHO NUMBER,
WHEN DATE, WHAT CHAR(40), BUDGET NUMBER,
SPENT NUMBER, TAX NUMBER);



INSERT INTO ADVERT SELECT * FROM TEMP;



DELETE FROM TEMP;



DROP TABLE TEMP;
```

Figure 10.3   Adding a new field to the ADVERT table.

(usually the default is very large). Alternately, a length may be specified enclosed in parentheses:

CREATE TABLE MYTABLE (MYFIELD NUMBER(6));

Here the field will be allowed to contain any number not exceeding six digits, including digits following the decimal point. A maximum may also be assigned to the number of digits allowed to follow the decimal point, by writing a second number preceded by a comma:

CREATE TABLE MYTABLE (MYFIELD NUMBER(8,3));

This statement declares that MYFIELD may contain no more than eight digits, and that three of those digits will appear after the decimal point. In other words, the number will have 000000.000 as a minimum and 999999.999 as a maximum.

The possible numeric field types specified by ANSI are NUMERIC, DECI-MAL, DEC (a synonym for DECIMAL), INTEGER, INT (a synonym for INTE-GER), SMALLINT, FLOAT, REAL, and DOUBLE PRECISION. The distinctions specified by this collection are primarily in *relative* size, and even this will depend not only upon the specific database implementation, but also on the actual computer upon which the database is running. For instance, a SMALLINT is defined to be *not larger than* an INTEGER, and a DOUBLE PRECISION is to be *larger than* a REAL.

10.6   Changing Table Structure

Although it is not included in the standard, some SQL implementations will allow existing tables to be changed with the ALTER TABLE syntax. The only type of change which may be effected with this command is to *add* a field to a table:

ALTER TABLE MYTABLE ADD FIELD2 NUMBER;

This statement will add a column to the MYTABLE table. The column and its fields will be named FIELD2 and the data type will be numeric. The field name, of course, must differ from any existing field name in that table. When the new column is created, all of its fields will be null.

Can a table structure be altered in the absence of the ALTER TABLE syntax? Can a field be *removed* from a table? Can a table be split, with half of its fields moving to a second table, and half moving to a third? Could two tables be combined, making one? All of these things can be done with variations of the statements used in Figure 10.3. Temporary tables are created to hold the data that is to reside in a new table structure. The data is moved to temporary storage. The original table is destroyed, and then recreated, using the new table structure. The data is then moved back into the redesigned original table. The temporary tables are then discarded.

10.7   Deleting Tables

Tables may be removed from the database with the simple words DROP
TABLE. The words are followed by the name of the table to be destroyed:

    DROP TABLE MYTABLE;

SQL will remove a table only if it contains no data, only if it is empty.
Before a table can be deleted, all records within that table must be deleted.

11. Privileges

Praise the mountains but love the plains.

GRANT ALL PRIVILEGES ON ALL_DATA TO FEW;

11.1   Responsibilities

You are not alone. Database installations are rarely accessible to only a single individual. Even single-user systems on microcomputers will be used at different times by different persons. Larger systems may be responding to dozens or even hundreds of users simultaneously. When you enter a database system, or *logon*, you will be asked to identify yourself by name and, often, by password. After the system has verified your identity and allowed you access to the database, any object which you create, whether a table or a view, will, internally, be stamped with your name. The object will *belong* to you. You, and you alone, will be allowed to add to, remove from, change, and view the contents of that object. Should other users know of the existence of your table, and even know its name, the database system will not allow them access to it unless you have registered your consent. Having created an object within the database, you have sole responsibility for determining who shall be allowed to do what with that object.

An important part of any database system is the proper distribution of responsibility. Much information will be of use to everyone, and therefore the right to *see* the tables containing that information will need to be widely distributed. The right to *add* data to important tables will be given only to those stalwarts responsible for data entry. The right to *remove* important data should be granted to the smallest possible number of people.

11.2   Granting Privileges

In the relational realm, rights and responsibilities are called *privileges*, and there are four of them: SELECT, INSERT, DELETE, and UPDATE. The giving of these privileges to others is called *granting*. You may grant, regarding any database object which belongs to you, any of the four privileges to any user of the database system. In addition, you may grant the *right to grant*, you may authorize a user to pass granted privileges along to other users.

The SQL verb which assigns privileges is GRANT. It is immediately followed by a list of the privileges being granted, or by the words ALL PRIVILEGES. The privileges are followed by the word ON, which introduces the name of the table or view to which the privileges apply:

grant all privileges on MYTABLE . . . ;

If privileges are listed individually, they are separated by commas:

grant select, insert on MYTABLE . . . ;

The words ALL PRIVILEGES may be shortened to ALL:

grant all on MYTABLE . . . ;

The UPDATE privilege may be restricted to specified fields, in which case the field names are listed, enclosed in parentheses and separated by commas:

grant update (FIELDA, FIELDC) on MYTABLE . . . ;

The users to whom the privileges are being granted are introduced by the word TO and are listed, by name, and separated by commas:

grant select, insert on MYTABLE to JENNIFER, MARK;

If privileges are to be assigned to *all* users, the single word PUBLIC may be used:

grant select, insert on MYTABLE to public;

Users who are granted privileges may be given the right to pass those privileges on to other users by appending the words WITH GRANT OPTION to the end of the GRANT statement:

grant select on MYTABLE to JENNIFER with grant option;

Any combination of privileges may be granted to any combination of users.

If all of our tables had been created by our database administrator, she might grant full rights to all users with statements like the following:

GRANT ALL ON MOONS TO PUBLIC;

GRANT ALL ON PEOPLE TO PUBLIC;

GRANT ALL ON UNITS TO PUBLIC;

She might allow users to change only the profession or birth-date fields in the personnel table with the statement:

GRANT UPDATE (PROF, BIRTH) ON PEOPLE TO PUBLIC;

Or perhaps only certain users might be allowed such rights:

GRANT UPDATE (PROF, BIRTH) ON PEOPLE
TO MARGARET, DAISY, JONATHAN;

Or she might designate one user to pass privileges on to other users:

GRANT ALL ON MOONS TO ELIZABETH
WITH GRANT OPTION;

Those doing data entry would need, of course, the INSERT privilege, and should be able to view the table, and might be granted the right to alter only certain fields:

GRANT INSERT, SELECT,
UPDATE (WHEN, WHAT, SPENT, TAX)
ON ADVERT TO
CONNIE, LANCE;

DesignNote: Enforcement of security within a database should combine the selective granting of privileges with the creation of views. Since particular fields may be specified only in conjunction with the UPDATE privilege, granting the SELECT privilege to only certain fields within a table would require that first a view be created, a view which included *only* those fields to which the privilege is to be granted.

Full Table Names

In the relational model, each user is looked upon as, in effect, controlling a separate database. The user's database consists of all tables and views created by that user. The ANSI standard designates these separate databases as *schemas*. The rules which enforce the uniqueness of database object *names* apply separately within each user's schema. In other words, user *John* may have a table named MYTABLE and user *Mary* may have a table with the same name. If John were to grant to Mary privileges over his table, how would Mary refer to that table in her select statements? She could not simply use the table name MYTABLE because the database would take that to mean *her* table of that name. She would need to use a *full table name*, which consists of the table name joined to an *authorization identifier*. The authorization identifier is, typically, the name of the user who owns the table. The full table name is formed by joining the table name to the authorization identifier, using a period:

john.mytable

mary.mytable

Mary would select from John's table with statements such as:

SELECT * FROM JOHN.MYTABLE;

Full table names will, of course, be accepted by the database system only if the user has been granted privileges over the designated table.

11.3   Revoking Privileges

Strange to tell, the ANSI standard provides no way of removing privileges once they have been granted. Commercial implementations have, however, generally settled upon the verb REVOKE. The syntax following the verb is identical to that of the GRANT syntax, with the only difference being that the user names are introduced by the word FROM rather than TO:

REVOKE ALL ON PEOPLE FROM MARGARET;

REVOKE INSERT, UPDATE ON MOONS
FROM MARK, ELIZABETH;

The WITH GRANT OPTION phrase, of course, is not used with the REVOKE operation.

12. The Catalog

Just scales and full measure injure no man.

SELECT ACCURACY FROM MEASUREMENT;

12.1 Looking It Up

"You can extract all data knowing only the verb *select*, the table names and field names..." Sounds familiar, doesn't it? Sounds simple. But what if you're a new user on a large system and, although you've a good idea what sort of *information* is to be found in the database, you really haven't a clue what the table names are, let alone the names of the fields within those tables? Or what if you are alone with your own, well-known system, one which contains hundreds of tables, all of which you yourself created, but many of which you created *months* ago, and whose names have not lingered in your head? You could of course write down the names of tables and their fields as you create them, but since computerized information stores are expressly intended to eliminate the need for such paper files, it would seem somewhat self-defeating. You could create a table within which you could record the names of tables and their fields. But surely the system itself has somewhere recorded the names of all tables that have been created, and the names of the fields within those tables; had it not done so, it would not be able to respond to your queries, for your queries reference things by name.

A relational database system does of course store the names of all tables and views as they are created. It stores the names of all the fields associated

SELECT TNAME, TYPE FROM SYSTABLES;

TNAME	TYPE
TABLES	TABLE
UNITS	TABLE
ADVERT	TABLE
PEOPLE	TABLE
SPENT	VIEW
CITY	TABLE
BUDGET	VIEW
DUMMY	TABLE
MONTH	TABLE
S_SYSTEM	TABLE
OUTER	VIEW
STATE	TABLE
CITY_STATE	VIEW
MP	VIEW
NAME_PLACE	VIEW
MOONS	TABLE

Figure 12.1   A hypothetical catalog.

with these database objects. It stores the names of the user who created the object along with the name of the object. It also stores other necessary bits of information about these objects, information which it uses to maintain the objects within the database. All of this information is stored just as user-created objects are, in the only way in which anything may be stored in a relational database, as *tables*.

These tables, which are created by and maintained by the system itself, are called *system tables* and the collection of all these tables is referred to as the system *catalog*. Since they are tables, they can be accessed just as any other table would be, using ordinary select statements. Within certain constraints, they may also be updated using normal SQL. Through queries to the catalog, the user should be able to look up the names of every table and view in the system, the names of every field contained within those objects, and additional information. Since the catalog is automatically maintained by the system, it will always be available and will always accurately reflect the status of the system at the present moment.

```
SELECT NAME, TNAME, TYPE FROM SYSCOLUMNS
ORDER BY TNAME;
```

NAME	TNAME	TYPE
WHO	ADVERT	NUMBER
WHEN	ADVERT	DATE
WHAT	ADVERT	CHARACTER
BUDGET	ADVERT	NUMBER
SPENT	ADVERT	NUMBER
TAX	ADVERT	NUMBER
ID	CITY	NUMBER
NAME	CITY	CHARACTER
STATE	CITY	CHARACTER
ID	DUMMY	NUMBER
⋮	⋮	⋮
ID	S_SYSTEM	NUMBER
NAME	S_SYSTEM	CHARACTER
DISTANCE	S_SYSTEM	NUMBER
DIAMETER	S_SYSTEM	NUMBER
⋮	⋮	⋮

Figure 12.2   System storage of field names.

12.2   Catalog Names

The ANSI standard makes no mention of the catalog, and commercial relational database implementations have gone their own ways in choosing names for the system tables. Therefore, the user will be forced to go to the reference manuals for the particular system in order to look up the naming conventions for the system tables. With any luck there will be one system table which contains the names of all other system tables, along with a brief description of what each table contains. If such a table exists the user need only remember that one table name, for through it all other system table names may be found at any time. Since there are no standards for system table names, there are of course no standards for field names within those tables. The names used in this chapter are hypothetical.

The catalog will reside in a schema created by and belonging to the system itself, and its tables will probably have to be accessed using full table names:

```
SELECT NAME FROM SYS.SYSCOLUMNS
WHERE TNAME = 'PEOPLE';
```

It may be necessary for the database administrator to grant privileges on the catalog tables to users who wish to see them.

12.3   Changing the Catalog

The catalog cannot be changed. The DML verbs INSERT, UPDATE, and DELETE cannnot be used with the catalog tables. All changes to the catalog are made by the system. The system executes a number of INSERT statements to the catalog whenever a new table is created, and likewise executes a number of DELETE statements when a table is dropped.

Catalog tables include text fields which contain descriptions of, or comments upon, the objects named in the catalog. Your database implementation should provide some syntax for adding and changing these text fields. The most commonly used syntax for this purpose is:

```
comment on table MYTABLE is 'This is a comment';
```

Comments should be added to the catalog whenever a new table is created:

```
COMMENT ON TABLE MOONS
IS 'The satellites of all solar system planets';
```

The system should also allow you to add comments to each column name:

```
COMMENT ON COLUMN MOONS.DISTANCE
IS 'Distance from the planet, in kilometers';
```

DesignNote: It should be mandatory for database administrators to add comments to every table name which they create, and to all column names within those tables. Users should be encouraged to add comments to the tables which they create. Comments will serve as an audit trail, a history, and a nudge to the memory. Although system structure should always be documented on paper, on "hard copy," such documentation can be misplaced. The comments within the catalog cannot be lost unless the system itself is lost.

13. The Dummy Table

There was never a good knife made of bad steel.

SELECT TOOLS FROM TRAINING;

13.1 A Tool for All Seasons

The dummy table is an instance of good things coming in small packages. It is a table of only one record, with that record containing only a single field. It has nothing whatever to do with the ANSI standard. It is created by us, to our liking, for our use. Once it has been created, and its one field has been filled (or not filled, as you wish), it will never be altered, it will never be operated upon by the DML verbs. But it will do good service. It will be there to be called upon in many different circumstances.

It is with the dummy table that we take what is given to us, by ANSI and by our particular database implementation, and, albeit in a small way, begin to create what is never given to us, our own chest of tools, implements to meet our needs and to be passed on to others to meet their needs. It is the construction, cataloging, and melding of these individual, or "site-specific" tools which will mark the success or failure of a database implementation.

We can create our tool with the following statement:

CREATE TABLE DUMMY (ID NUMBER);

The table could be given any name. The name DUMMY is meant to convey the fact that this table is used to do things which do not require the services of a "real" table. Since in the relational universe, there can be no objects other than tables, and since all actions must be actions upon these objects, we shall have a "fake" table, a "dummy," with which we can perform non-table actions. The table's single field could of course be given any name. We can fill the table with the following command:

INSERT INTO DUMMY VALUES (0);

This is entirely arbitrary. As we shall see, the field could be left null, or filled with any value. No matter.

13.2   Doing Arithmetic

One of the things that we shall use the dummy table for is to do arithmetic. The table shall not do the arithmetic. The table will in fact have nothing to do with the calculations. It will merely serve as sort of an "excuse" for requesting arithmetic calculations from the database.

SQL and its SELECT verb may be used to query the database for a *constant*, a numeric value, either simple or calculated. The value is *not* taken from a value within a table, but is derived from information given in the SELECT statement itself:

SELECT 25 FROM DUMMY;

The above statement will return the number *25*. This is not terribly useful. Before we make it more useful, let's note *why* we are selecting our constant from the DUMMY table, rather than from some other table. The statement below would also return the number *25*:

SELECT 25 FROM S_SYSTEM;

But it would return the number *ten times*, once for each row in the S_SYSTEM table. Since we have specified no WHERE clause, restricting which rows are to be selected, *all* rows will be selected, and the constant will be returned once for each row. This is the point of the DUMMY table; it has only *one* row. When we request that the database deliver to us a constant, and name the DUMMY table as the vehicle to be used, we can be certain that we will receive the constant once and only once.

Now that we know *why* we are going to select constants from the DUMMY table, we can select more useful constants. If we knew that one kilometer were equal to 0.6214 mile, and we wanted to find some number that we could multiply kilometers by in order to convert to miles, we could query the following:

SELECT (1 / 0.6214) FROM DUMMY;

The database would deliver the number 1.6, which we could then use to derive kilometers from miles:

SELECT (250 * 1.6) FROM DUMMY;

SELECT (12 − 34 + 89 − 56 + 107) FROM DUMMY;

$$\frac{(12-34+89-56+107)}{118}$$

SELECT ((23.5 * 38.73) / (9.34 + 7.97)) FROM DUMMY;

$$\frac{((23.5*38.73)/(9.34+7.97))}{52.5797227}$$

Figure 13.1   Doing arithmetic.

The above query would inform us that 250 miles are equivalent to 400 kilometers.

The complexity of the arithmetic expressions which may be presented in a query will be limited only by the capacity of your particular database implementation, but in theory there is no limit:

SELECT
((250 * 1.6) / ((89.234 + 35.43) * (123 * 35.5)))
FROM DUMMY;

Once it is created, the DUMMY table will always be available, enlisting the database system as a pocket calculator.

13.3   Applications

The DUMMY table's usefulness extends beyond mere arithmetic. It will find a small but important role in certain SQL database *applications*, such as *forms*. Applications are entirely outside the ANSI standard specification, but they will prove to be the bulk of the work done by database administrators and programmers. In an application which implements forms, and perhaps in other applications, depending upon the particular database implementation, there will be *variables*, essentially individual fields which exist within the application but entirely outside the database, fields which can be used to store values which will be used within the application. It will be necessary, during the execution of the application to store values within these variables, or to change values which are already there. In a forms application, it will likely be the case that values can be moved only though the use of valid SQL statements. In other words, if we wanted to set a variable X to a value of zero, we would *not* be able to say something as straightforward as:

$$\text{let } X = 0$$

We would only be allowed to fill the variable through the use of a SQL statement, and would be allowed one additional word in the vocablulary, most likely the word *into*, which would be used to introduce the name of the variable to be acted upon. We would want to select a constant value, zero, and move it into our variable, and we would want to be sure that this value was moved once and only once, which is just what the DUMMY table allows us to do:

SELECT 0 INTO X FROM DUMMY;

We might, later in our application, find a need to move the value 100 into the variable Y:

SELECT 100 INTO Y FROM DUMMY;

The DUMMY table again stands ready for use in small but vital tasks.

14. The Temp Table

By doing nothing we learn to do ill.

CREATE TABLE TEMP (THIS_JOB CHAR,
THAT_JOB NUMBER, NEXT_JOB CHAR);

14.1 Made to Order

The TEMP table is a chameleon. Unlike the lizard, it does not merely change its color. It passes out of existence and is reborn in another guise. Again and again. It is brought into being in the form which is required at a particular time, and, having done its duty, is discarded, only to be marshaled once more at another time. It is temporary. It may serve as a holding bin, where data might be tucked away for a moment, on its way to a new permanent home. It may serve as a scratch pad, where new manipulations may be tried on old data. It might live for a time as a classroom, where a hesitant user could explore the features of SQL without fear of doing damage.

The TEMP table, or some other temporary, discardable table, should *always* be used whenever trials or experiments are attempted. No user or administrator is or ever will be sufficiently infallible to attempt new and potentially damaging procedures upon "production" data. The relational architecture's flexibility in creating new database objects, or in copying old ones, should be used to bring into existence new, non-vital playing fields where procedures can be "burned in" and perfected. It can not be too greatly emphasized that vast amounts of damage can be done, hundreds of hours of work can be lost, with a simple SQL "slip of the tongue," with the wrong verb used on the wrong table. Temporary tables should be made to stand guard over the database, along with views and privileges.

The TEMP table is an application of SQL and has nothing whatever to do with the ANSI standard. It is simply a table which will be created, using the CREATE verb, whenever a temporary table is needed, in whatever form it is needed. It will then be discarded:

DELETE FROM TEMP;

DROP TABLE TEMP;

We used the TEMP table in the chapter on table creation in order to tamporarily hold a table's data while we altered the structure of the table. You will find many uses for this table and it should be freely discarded and remade as need warrants.

14.2   The ID Field

We have built into a number of our tables a field which contains, for each record, an arbitrary, unique number, to be used as a JOIN COLUMN when connecting records in one table to records in another table. But how is this field to be maintained? How is a person doing data entry to know *what* number to place into each new record? The number must be unique within that table, but there could be thousands of records already entered; hundreds of records may have been deleted, and hundreds more added.

If we were limited to "straight" SQL, with all of its limitations; if we were unable to use a *form* or some other automated device; well, then it would be somewhat complex and convoluted to maintain an ID field. But let us do it nevertheless, as an exercise, and to illustrate some of the weaknesses of SQL as it is defined in the standard.

Under all circumstances, we will be faced with a two-step procedure. We will first enter a new record to the table, including all data *except* the ID value. We will then find and enter an appropriate ID value for that record. It will not be possible to do all of this with a single INSERT statement.

Let's first add a record and its id in a way using syntax which is not included in the ANSI standard but which has been implemented in some commercial database systems. We will add a new record to the CITY table:

INSERT INTO CITY VALUES (−1, 'Baltimore', 'MD');

We have created a new record and filled its ID field, temporarily, with a value of negative one. The −1 is, of course, not the id which we want to leave this record with. It is, in fact, an illegal id (no negative numbers allowed). We are using the negative value as a unique *marker*, so that we can find and alter the one record which we have just created:

```
UPDATE CITY SET ID =
(SELECT (MAX(ID) + 1) FROM CITY)
WHERE ID = -1;
```

The above statement, although it would be accepted in some commercial SQL implementations, is *illegal within the ANSI standard*. The standard does not allow a SELECT statement to be the right-hand term in a SET clause. But let's accept the syntax and see if it accomplishes what we wish to have done. Will the above statement assign to the newly created *Baltimore, MD* record an id number which is unique within the CITY table? It will do so, for it first finds the highest number within the ID column (max(id)), then adds one to that number, and assigns the result to the newly created record. It is *not possible* that a record within the CITY table could contain an id value which is higher than the highest value; therefore the number calculated by our statement *cannot already exist* within the CITY table; therefore it must be unique.

> *DesignNote:* The above procedure is not foolproof. What if step one were executed, and not step two, leaving a record with an id of −1? The next time the procedure were executed, a *second* record would be created with an id of −1, and then, in the second part of the procedure, *both* records so marked would be given the newly calculated id. In this way duplicate id numbers could creep into the table. The prevention of duplicates must be done by combining intelligent data entry procedures with preventive table *design*. Had the CITY table been created with its ID field designated UNIQUE it would not be possible to enter duplicate numbers, mistakenly or otherwise; the database system would not allow it.

Within the Standard

Is there some way to maintain the ID field without violating SQL syntax as defined in the ANSI standard? There is and we shall do it here, but we shall find that the procedure must be even more convoluted than the one above. The ANSI definition of the SQL language leaves much to be desired.

First let us create a table identical to the CITY table:

```
CREATE TABLE TEMP
(ID NUMBER, NAME CHAR(40),
STATE CHAR(2));
```

The procedure will involve building just a single record in the TEMP table and then transferring that record to the CITY table. Since, as we shall see, it will be vitally important that there be only a single record in the TEMP table at any given time, we will begin the procedure by ensuring that *no* records exist in the TEMP table:

DELETE FROM TEMP;

The above statement will leave the TEMP table empty. We will now reverse our previous procedure, and create a record with *only* the ID field filled:

INSERT INTO TEMP (ID)
SELECT (MAX(ID) + 1) FROM CITY;

We now have, in the TEMP table, one record, and its id field contains a number which is *unique* both for the TEMP table (since it is the *only* record there) and for the CITY table. We can now enter our data:

UPDATE TEMP
SET NAME = 'Baltimore',
STATE = 'MD'
WHERE ID IS NOT NULL;

The WHERE clause in the above statement is, of course, unnecessary, since there is only one record in the TEMP table. Only that one record can be updated. Better safe than sorry. We have now completed a new record for the CITY table, with a unique id number, but the record is in the TEMP table. We must now move it to where it belongs:

INSERT INTO CITY
SELECT * FROM TEMP;

The above statement will move *all* records in the TEMP table to the CITY table. But there is only the one record, so only it will be moved. The one record contains the new data for the CITY table and is stamped with an id number which will be unique within the CITY table. The first step in repeating the procedure would be to delete the one record from the TEMP table.

The above procedure could be executed any number of times, adding any number of new records to the CITY table, and each record would be added with a unique id number. The procedure is, of course, rather tedious. It demonstrates both the weakness of the SQL language and its strength—after all, we *did* do it. In the "real" world, the world of commercial database implementations, there would be utilities, such as *forms*, which would allow the database administrator to automate the above procedures, so that data entry personnel would merely enter "Baltimore" and "MD" and the utility would, behind the scenes, calculate a unique id and assign it to the new record.

15. Forms

Straight trees have crooked roots.

SELECT PRESENTATION
FROM PREPARATIONS
WHERE DISPLAY =
'UNCLUTTERED';

15.1   Selecting Without SQL

SQL is all well and good, especially for those who are proficient in it—you can sit at your computer terminal and, with just a few typed words, bring forth from a vast assortment of data just the bits and pieces you care to see, in just the order in which you care to see them. Or you can playfully probe, looking here and there, finding this interesting thing and that uninteresting item. But what of those who are *not* versed in SQL? Are their terminals to be roadblocks to the database rather than access routes? And what of the SQL master, who must today, as on all days, check the same data, type the same SQL statements? Whether because you know SQL not at all or because you know it all too well, there will be times when you will simply not care to be bothered with it. Thus was invented the FORM.

A form is simply an application which draws a picture upon a computer terminal. The picture will contain, at specific locations upon the screen, fields which will correspond to fields within one or more tables from the database. The fields upon the screen will be filled with data extracted from the database, or, conversely, fields within the database will be updated with

109

*** DATA ENTRY — PERSONNEL ***

Use: the F1 key to view a record
        the F2 key to create a record

First Name: _____

Last Name: _____

Profession: _____

Birth: __—__—__ (enter as dd—mmm—yy)

City: _____

Figure 15.1   A typical form.

---

entries made to the fields of the form. A form will also display headings
and labels and directions for its use. It is the labels and the preset and
unchanging arrangement of the fields upon the screen that distinguishes a
form from the ad hoc use of SQL.

How forms are created is beyond the scope of this book, for one simple
reason: The *how* will vary with every vendor's database implementation.
The means of creating forms will be as manifold as the applications em-
bodying those means. There are no standards here, and likely there never
will be.

But, as in all implementations of SQL, as in all computer applications of
any kind, *techniques* will hold; the tricks useful in one vendor's application
will prove useful, perhaps with modification, in another's.

We will walk through a particular problem and its solution which will illustrate a number of the problems and possibilities which you will encounter
in using any forms package.

15.2   Into

Applications such as a form will provide to the user something which cannot
exist in a relational database: an object that may be used to store data
but which is *not* a table. These objects, which are essentially individual,
free-standing fields, will be created within the form and can be used to

hold data while the form application is executing. The application should allow data to be selected from these fields just as data may be selected from tables. The syntax should be the same. But moving data *into* these fields will require new syntax. The most commonly used word for this purpose is INTO, which will introduce the names of the form fields into which selected data is be placed:

select FIELDA into FIELDX from MYTABLE ...

If we had created within our form two-character fields, named FORM_FNAME and FORM_LNAME, of sufficient length, we might fill them with the following statement:

```
SELECT FNAME, LNAME
INTO FORM_FNAME, FORM_LNAME
FROM PEOPLE
WHERE LNAME = 'Mallory';
```

If we had within our form a field called FORM_NUM we might fill it with a constant value by executing the following statement:

```
SELECT 250
INTO FORM_NUM
FROM DUMMY;
```

We now have a way of storing bits and pieces of tables, as well as constant values, *outside* of the database structure. The data in our form fields will exist and can be used only so long as the form application is executing.

Data which is entered into the form on the computer screen will be deposited, by the forms application, into form fields. When the form is created, the designer will designate which internal form field is to receive the data entered in each of the displayed fields.

15.3   The Trigger

Forms on a computer screen are filled in in a certain *order*. First one displayed field is filled in, then another, and so on, in an order which is designated by the person who designs the form. What concerns us here is what happens *before and after* each field is filled in by the user. When a forms application is executed, when it "runs," the first thing it does is draw a picture on the computer screen, similar, perhaps, to the one in Figure 15.1. The next action it takes which is *visible to the user* is to prompt the user to fill in a field. After this, it will visibly prompt the user for the next field, and so on. Before and after each of these prompts, the application may be taking actions "behind the scenes," invisible to the user.

The actions which a form may take before and after prompting for data will vary with the particular database implementation, but these possible actions will certainly include SQL statements, statements acting upon both database tables and fields local to the form. The form designer will designate what actions are to be taken before and after each displayed field is filled in. These actions are often called *triggers*, because they are triggered by actions taken on the displayed form. There will be *pre-entry* tirggers and *post-entry* triggers, actions which will take place *before* and *after* each displayed field is filled.

A pre-entry or post-entry trigger could be any number of SQL statements, statements which acted upon any table in the database. The statements might select data from the database tables and move that data into form fields, or they might move data from the fields within the form into fields within database tables. The triggers could update existing database records, create new ones, or even create new tables. A forms application should allow the designer to build triggers which can do anything which is allowed within SQL.

15.4   The ID Field

A form is precisely the sort of automated application that we need to maintain the ID fields which we have built into a number of our tables. The ID field functions as a JOIN COLUMN and is used to link records in one table to records in other tables. A record's id is simply a number, entirely random except for the fact that it must be *unique* within its table. No two records in a given table may have the same id number. When a new record is created, using the INSERT verb, a unique id must be assigned to it, and that number must be placed in the record's ID field.

A form allows us to effortlessly and transparently calculate new id values and assign them to records created through the form. Assume that the form in Figure 15.1 were to be used to add new records to our PEOPLE table. There is no field on the form in which a data entry person might enter an id number for newly created records. This is exactly the point—using a form, the data entry staff need *never know of the existence* of the ID field.

Our form will contain a local numeric field called FORM_ID and it will contain a pre-entry trigger, a trigger which will execute before the first displayed field is entered by the user. The trigger will execute the following statement:

```
SELECT (MAX(ID) + 1)
INTO FORM_ID
FROM PEOPLE;
```

The statement finds the highest id number in the PEOPLE table, adds one to it, and then deposits the resulting number into the FORM_ID field. This number is guaranteed to be unique for the PEOPLE table, since no id number there can be greater than the greatest one. With the execution of this trigger, there exists within the form application, and entirely unknown to the user, a number which can be used to fill the ID field in the next record which is added to the PEOPLE table.

Using similar triggers we could take the name of the city entered in the form and look up in the CITY table the id of the city and the abbreviation of its state name. These values could be placed into form fields named FORM_CITY and FORM_STATE, to be used when creating a new record for the PEOPLE table.

When the user has filled in all the fields of the form in Figure 15.1, and wishes to create a new record, a trigger containing the following statement would execute:

```
INSERT INTO PEOPLE VALUES
(FORM_ID, FORM_FNAME, FORM_LNAME, FORM_PROF,
FORM_BIRTH, FORM_CITY, FORM_STATE);
```

Using a form such as the one we have described, the data entry staff could enter record after record into the PEOPLE table without ever being aware of the existence of the records' id values, or of the numbers placed into the CITY column, or of the abbreviations placed into the STATE column. Forms allow us to leave the database mechanisms in the background, unseen.

15.5   Searching for Strings

Forms are often used to find already existing data, rather than to create new data. We might tell users that the form in Figure 15.1 could be used to locate the record of any individual simply by filling in the last name field. We might then execute a trigger which would select from the PEOPLE table using that one bit of information:

```
SELECT FNAME, LNAME, PROF, BIRTH
INTO FORM_FNAME, FORM_LNAME, FORM_PROF,
FORM_BIRTH FROM PEOPLE
WHERE LNAME = FORM_LNAME;
```

We might inform them that they could enter even partial names, and that the form would find an individual's record if the letters which were entered existed within the person's name. We could do this using SQL's partial string operator, the percent sign (%). In other words, if the user were to enter the string "%allo%" our form would then go off and find the record for "Mallory." The problem with this is twofold: 1, users who are not familiar with the ways of SQL will not care to be bothered with having to enter strange things like percent signs; 2, administrators will not care to have to explain to every user the how and why of using the percent sign operator. It would be most convenient if we could allow the user to enter just any old name, or partial name, without having to worry about special characters.

Concatenation

A forms application will contain many features and operators which do not exist in standard SQL. One of these will be an operator which performs *concatenation*. Concatenation is simply the joining of two or more character strings to form a single string. Since the ANSI standard specifies no concatenation operator, the syntax will most likely vary from one commercial implementation to another. We will use a double ampersand (&&) as our operator. Using the concatenation operator we could write:

    ... 'string one' && ' ' && 'string two' ...

The result of this operation would be one long string combining the three shorter strings:

    ... 'string one string two' ...

We can now use this operator to make things a little easier for the user who is searching for personnel records through a form.

The user could be allowed to enter the string "allo" into the last name field of the form, and request that a record be found. Our forms application would take the partial string, and, using the concatenation operator, would compose an SQL statement that would search the LNAME column of the PEOPLE table:

    SELECT FNAME, LNAME, PROF, BIRTH
    INTO FORM_FNAME, FORM_LNAME, FORM_PROF,
    FORM_BIRTH FROM PEOPLE
    WHERE LNAME = ('%' && FORM_LNAME && '%');

This statement would result in a search being made for the string "%allo%" and this would result in the name "Mallory" being found.

With the use of a very simple operator we have eliminated the need for our forms users to know anything about special SQL characters such as the percent sign.

Which Substring?

Now the fun begins. Our problem is hardly solved. Let us imagine that our PEOPLE table is much larger than it is, containing hundreds of names. Imagine that the table contains both the name "goldstein" and the name "stein" (let us ignore upper and lower case letters for this little demonstration). Suppose that our user enters "stein" into the form and requests a search. Our application will do its concatenation and will do a select using "%stein%" in its WHERE clause. What happens if SQL, in the course of its search, comes across the name "goldstein" *before* it finds the record with "stein" in its LNAME field?

TechNote: When searching for partial strings, SQL cannot use indexes. It must look through records sequentially, one at a time, and test each for the existence of the partial string. The partial string could occur anywhere in the field being searched; at the very beginning, in the middle, or at the very end. Indexes are useful only if you know how the string *begins*. Since the search must be done sequentially, and since records in a relational database table are *unordered*, there is no way of knowing whether "stein" or "goldstein" will be the first to be matched.

SQL would declare that "goldstein" is a match, since it contains the substring "stein," and it would deliver to the form the "goldstein" record.

Why is this a problem? If our user wanted the record of someone whose full name was "stein," she simply would not be able to retrieve it. She could not specify the name any more completely and SQL would continue to find the "goldstein" record.

What to do? We must expand our trigger, using more than one SQL statement. We must in fact be prepared to perform more than a single search. We must: 1, check to see if there is an *exact* match for the string which the user entered; i.e., the user specified the name fully; 2, check to see if any name *begins* with the string which the user entered; 3, check to see if any name *contains*, anywhere within it, the string which was entered. Step two could be left out; we have put it in because it seems more natural that when a partial name is specified, names *beginning* with that substring should be preferred over names containing that substring elsewhere.

So we must be prepared, within our trigger to do three searches, one with each of the following WHERE clauses:

WHERE LNAME = FORM_LNAME;

WHERE LNAME = (FORM_LNAME && '%');

WHERE LNAME = ('%' && FORM_LNAME && '%');

This is not a problem, since a forms implemention should allow a trigger to contain any number of SQL statements. So we shall write all three statements into our trigger.

Alas, our problems are not at an end. Statements within a trigger execute one after another. What if "stein" is entered and our first trigger statement finds a match? Our second trigger statement will then proceed to execute and it too will find a match ("goldstein"). The third statement will then execute and it will also find "goldstein." Only the result of the *entire* trigger will be presented to our user. Again, she will be unable to find "stein." She will always be given "goldstein."

What to do? We must somehow set our trigger so that only *one* statement will retrieve data from the database. We must fix things so that once one statement has found a match, the subsequent statements will be *barred* from successful execution. We can do this by using a special numeric form

```
SELECT 0 INTO ON_OFF FROM DUMMY;

SELECT 1, FNAME, LNAME, PROF, BIRTH
INTO ON_OFF, FORM_FNAME, FORM_LNAME, FORM_PROF,
FORM_BIRTH FROM PEOPLE
WHERE (LNAME = FORM_LNAME
AND ON_OFF = 0);

SELECT 1, FNAME, LNAME, PROF, BIRTH
INTO ON_OFF, FORM_FNAME, FORM_LNAME, FORM_PROF,
FORM_BIRTH FROM PEOPLE
WHERE (LNAME = (FORM_LNAME && '%')
AND ON_OFF = 0);

SELECT 1, FNAME, LNAME, PROF, BIRTH
INTO ON_OFF, FORM_FNAME, FORM_LNAME, FORM_PROF,
FORM_BIRTH FROM PEOPLE
WHERE (LNAME = ('%' && FORM_LNAME && '%')
AND ON_OFF = 0);
```

Figure 15.2   A trigger that searches for substrings.

---

field. Assume that the forms designer has included in the form a numeric field called ON_OFF. The first thing we shall do in our trigger is set this field to "off":

```
SELECT 0 INTO ON_OFF FROM DUMMY;
```

Next we shall arrange that any successful select statement in the trigger will set the ON_OFF fiield to "on," and that the select statements will execute *only* if the field is "off":

```
SELECT 1, FNAME, LNAME, PROF, BIRTH
INTO ON_OFF, FORM_FNAME, FORM_LNAME, FORM_PROF,
FORM_BIRTH FROM PEOPLE
WHERE (LNAME = FORM_LNAME
AND ON_OFF = 0);
```

You can see what we have done (the full trigger is printed in Figure 15.2). The statement above will execute only if the ON_OFF field contains a zero, for that condition is specified in the WHERE clause. But if it executes successfully, if the ON-OFF field is zero *and* a match is found for the entered substring, then the statement will select the value *one* into the ON-OFF field, thus barring any similar statements from successful execution.

Our trigger is now fairly sophisticated. It allows a user to enter any combination of letters whatever and it performs up to three different searches in order to find the most rational fit for the entered string.

We have worked through this exercise to demonstrate some of the subtleties that will be encountered in designing SQL applications. The exact statements which we have used may not be acceptable in the database implementation which you are using, but it should be possible to employ the techniques in some way.

16. Reports

The brave man is the prudent one.

SELECT DOCUMENTATION FROM DISCOVERIES;

16.1   Writing it Down

Written reports have always been the tired and tireless products of our electronic information systems. They seem somehow embarrassing, the great anachronism that all the computerized wizardry was intended to replace, not produce. Conscientious staff devise elegant and ordered presentations of yesterday's achievements and tomorrow's hopes, left-justified here and decimal-aligned there, bordered and boxed in arrow-straight lines, inserted and footnoted, and... "sorry, but the president hasn't found time to look at it yet." Lying in folders and files, written reports are today's poor relations to the rainbow displays of the computer terminal. Yet they are here still. Musty and magnificent, they are the abiding reminder of where the wizardry came from. There is no end to them, nor should there be.

Finished reports seem deceptively simple. Neat and orderly rows and columns, headers and totals, sit so perfectly upon the page that it seems they were born there, that surely they dropped out of the database in just the way we see them. The truth is otherwise. The tools and techniques which are used in designing and creating "hard copy" are no less subtle and difficult than the ones which create and manage the database itself. Those who haven't had to do it will never appreciate the care and cunning which may be required for a thing so simple as finding an optimal page break. The column which a report lists and sums may contain more entries tomorrow than it does today; tomrrow's report will need to place the column just as neatly as did today's. Those who devise reports must have foresight as well as an intimate knowledge of the contents and structure of the database.

16.2   Variables

Reports, along with forms and programs, are distinguished from interactive SQL by their ability to crate and minipulate local *variables*. Variables are simply storage areas, created by the report application, which exist as long as the application is "running." Variables are very similar to database *fields*, but they are independent and free-standing, not belonging to a table or any other grouping. Each variable must, as fields must, have a particular data type, a type which is declared when the variable. is created.

Report "generators," commercial applications which a designer can use to create written documents, will be as varied as the companies offering them. ANSI speaks not of reports. They will all provide some means of "declaring" variables. The "command" words which declare variables and perform most other actions within a report application, are usually prefaced with an *escape character*, some special mark which tells the application that the word following the mark is a command to be acted upon, not merely a bit of text. The escape character will vary from implementation to implementation. We will use the *backslash* (\). The declaration, the creation, of variables within a report application would proceed as the following:

\DECLARE   TEMP   999999.99

\DECLARE   SPENT_TOTAL   999999.99

\DECLARE   LAST_NAME   T20

\DECLARE   FIRST_NAME   T15

We have created two numeric variables, each with two decimal places and a maximum value of 999,999.99, and two character variables, of lengths 15 and 20.

Variable are made to be manipulated, and the application will provide commands for moving constant values into our storage areas, and for doing arithmetic with numeric variables:

\SET   HEADER   'ADVERTISING DEPARTMENT EXPENSES'

\SET   TEMP   100

Here we have moved a string into the character variable HEADER and moved the value 100 into TEMP. Arithmetic operations will typically specify two variables to be acted upon and a third variable in which to store the result:

\ADD   SPENT   TEMP   SPENT_TOTAL

Here the value in numeric variable TEMP is added to the value in SPENT and the result is placed in the variable SPENT_TOTAL.

16.3 Into

Report generators also distinguish themselves from interactive SQL by adding a word to the language, INTO. The word is used within the report's SELECT statements to introduce the names of variables into which selected data will be placed. The syntax is as follows:

select FIELDA into VARIABLEA from TABLEA;

For each field selected there must be specified a variable to receive its data, and the data type of the variable must match the data type of the field supplying the data. The following statement, when executed, would draw data from the database into our local variables:

```
SELECT FNAME, LNAME
INTO FIRST_NAME, LAST_NAME
FROM PEOPLE;
```

We would now have two bits of information, taken from the database, wholly within our application. We can do with that data as we wish, without any further reference to the database.

16.4 Execution

Report generators will allow select statements to be associated with a particular name, so that the statement may be executed anywhere within the application by simply "calling" the name, without having to repeatedly write out the entire statement. We might reduce the above query to a single word with the following statement:

```
\DEFINE GET_NAME
SELECT FNAME, LNAME
INTO FIRST_NAME, LAST_NAME
FROM PEOPLE;
```

The word GET_NAME has been made to stand for an entire select statement. We could now execute that statement, at any time, pulling bits of data into our variables, by writing:

```
\EXECUTE GET_NAME
```

The maximum number of variables which may be declared and statements which may be defined will vary from one database implementation to another, and can actually prove inadequate in a large and complex report application.

ADVERTISING DEPARTMENT EXPENSES — January 1987

Name	Location	Expense
David Dryden	Denver Colorado	327.65
Advert Dept.		44.65
Advert Dept.		101.77
Lance Roberts	Flagstaff Arizona	443.09
Connie DeMarco	Chicago Illinois	106.73
Mary DeMott	Flagstaff Arizona	52.88
	TOTAL:	$ 1076.77

Figure 16.1   A simple report.

16.5   One Row at a Time

What truly distinguishes report applications from interactive SQL is the fact that any select statement, when executed, will return only a *single* row. In interactive SQL, as we have seen, all rows that satisfy the search criteria are splashed on the computer terminal. When a report application begins executing, the database is "pointed" at the first record of each table. Remember that the first record may be any record whatever, for rows within a table are *unordered*. If an unqualified SELECT statement, one with no WHERE clause, is issued, this first record, and only this record, will be returned.

After the database has complied with a SELECT statement's demands, by finding a single row and dropping its data into the local variables within the report application, the database will move its pointer, its place-marker, within the table, so that it points to the next row. This next row will be returned if the SELECT statement is executed again. One row at a time is returned, one with each execution of the query. In between queries the report application may manipulate and massage the data which it has already retrieved in whatever fashion it wishes. The report has the power to pause after each query, to look at and judge the data it has just received, or compare it to data previously selected, and then to decide a course of action.

The power to pause after each query is immeasurably enhanced by the fact that the report application may hold numerous different SELECT statements open at the same time, first fetching a row from one, then fetching two rows from another, and so on. The report can have its "hands" into many tables at the same time, or have many hands into the same table, with SELECT statements containing various WHERE clauses.

Flow Control

We can assign a name to particular lines within the report application, and direct the execution of statements to skip certain lines and resume at some other line. In this way the "flow" of the application can be altered and controlled. We can have the report flow *to* one SELECT statement and *around* another, and then have it flow through these queries in some different order.

A name which is assigned to a line of an application is called a *label*. It is simply a way of marking a particular point in the application so that it can easily be referred to. The syntax for declaring labels will vary with different database applications. We shall simply use the word "label" followed by the name which we wish to assign to that particular line:

\LABEL SECTION_A

\LABEL SUM_LOOP

Altering the flow of the application will usually fall to the word "goto." The word will be followed by the name of the line to which the flow is to be directed:

\GOTO SECTION_A

\GOTO SUM_LOOP

With labels and the simple verb "goto" we can repeatedly direct our application to the execution of a particular query, retrieving row after row of a certain table; we can have it jump to a special query only when certain conditions are met, and to yet another query under other conditions.

When to Goto

We will want to change the flow of our application only under certain circumstances, only when certain conditions have been met. We need to have some means of determining how things stand within the application at any given moment. The report generator will provide a number of "if" statements which will be used to test the values of local variables.

Normally, when a query fails to select a row, either because *no* rows meet the specified conditions or because the *last* row has already been selected, the application will fill the indicated local variables with a null value. We can test for this condition:

\IF_NULL LAST_NAME

The above statement would inform our application whether or not it had retrieved the final last name.

TechNote: A statement which tests for null is hardly foolproof. After all, the field within the table might legitimately contain a null, in which case having fetched a null would *not* indicate that the last row had been found. A way around this is to always fetch, along with the needed data, some field which is known to have been created NOT NULL. If *that* field is returned containing a null value, then it safely indicates that no row was found.

Other "if" statements will allow the application to test for particular values within local variables. As in SQL WHERE clauses, forms applications will be able to test for equality, less than, and greater than:

\IF SPENT_TOTAL = 5520

\IF TEMP > 100

\IF LAST_NAME = 'Mallory'

\IF TEMP <= 5

Conditions having been determined, the application proceeds to a certain line with the words "then goto" followed by a label:

\IF LAST_NAME = 'Mallory' THEN GOTO SECTION_A

\IF TEMP >= 200 THEN GOTO SUM_LOOP

\IF_NULL LAST_NAME THEN GOTO SECTION_B

Using labels and *goto* directives, report applications may be broken into logically ordered sections, with each section doing some piece of the whole job. Some sections will be subordinate to others, and will be "called" by the major sections when they are needed. Applications which are built in this way are known as *structured* applications.

```
\SET FIRST_NAME 'Jennifer'

\SET LAST_NAME 'Mallory'

\SET SPENT_TOTAL 0

\DEFINE PERSON_SUM
SELECT SPENT INTO TEMP
FROM ADVERT WHERE WHO =
(SELECT ID FROM PEOPLE WHERE
FNAME = FIRST_NAME AND
LNAME = LAST_NAME);

    ⋮

\LABEL SUM_LOOP

\EXECUTE PERSON_SUM

\IF_NULL TEMP GOTO END_LOOP

\ADD TEMP SPENT_TOTAL SPENT_TOTAL

\GOTO SUM_LOOP

\LABEL END_LOOP

    ⋮
```

Figure 16.2   Taking a sum within a report.

16.6   Formatting

Reports, of course, are intended to be printed. Report generators create computer files which are then sent to a printer for finished output. The report application will provide commands which embed within the file instructions for the printer, such as when to end the current page and begin a new one ("form-feed"); when to begin a new column of text ("tabs"); when to use boldface text; when to underline.

> *TechNote:* Breaking the page and starting a new one can be anything but trivial. The application must know how many lines of text will fit on the paper which is to be used in printing. It must keep a count of text lines as it writes them to the file. These things are simple. What is *not* so simple are things like totals and subtotals. You cannot run a column of numbers down a page and have the total appear all alone on the *next* page. The application must not only know which line of the page it is currently writing to, it must also be aware of how many lines remain. When the end of a page is near, the application must be able to "look ahead" and determine if a total, or some other summary information, will be necessary and whether or not it will fit on the current page.

Commands will be included for manipulating strings. It will be possible to concatenate strings, bringing several small ones together to make a more easily managed single string:

\SET FULL_NAME FIRST_NAME && LAST_NAME

The command repertoire may allow strings to be changed to upper case, or to lower case. It may be possible to set only the first character in a string to upper case. Operators may be provided which search for and extract selected *parts* of strings.

Report generators vary from the subtle and sophisticated to the crude and clumsy. With the less advanced applications, it may be necessary to generate the report file and to then further refine that file using a word processing program.

> *DesignNote:* The administrator of a database installation must be well aware of the kinds of written reports that will be expected from the system. The design of tables can hang on something as seemingly unrelated as the size of paper which is to be used for reports. If a text field in a table is longer than the width of the paper, it will not be possible to incorporate that field in written reports. The capabilities of the report generator included in the system must also be taken into account. If it allows text to be converted from lower to upper case, or vice versa, then the text can be entered into tables in whatever case is

convenient. If this capability is not provided, it may be necessary to enter data into tables in the form in which it is to appear in written reports.

16.7   Import, Export

There is more than one way to fill a table. Great amounts of information may be moved into the database system without the use of data entry staff. This data will be brought into the computer in the form of a *file*. The file will then be read by a database utility program, which will take the data from the file and deposit it in designated tables. This process of filling tables from a file which is external to the database is called the *import* of data. The opposite process, that of taking data from the database and writing it to a file, is called the *export* of data. The difference between writing a report and exporting data is that exported data is not formatted for printing and the file contains no special commands for the printer. Exported data is simply data and is not for human consumption; an export file is intended only for a computer to read.

Using export and import utilities, data may be moved from a database on one computer to a database on another computer. The exported file is moved to the second computer, using a floppy diskette, a modem, or some other transfer device, and the file is then imported into the second database. Government and research organizations often sell data in a file format which is suitable for importing into a relational database.

Report writing utilities may be used to export data. If *no* formatting commands are used and the data is spaced properly, a file suitable for import may be created. An export utility will normally be restricted to exporting data from only a single table at a time. By employing the report writer as an export program, data from any number of tables can be combined and exported in a form which will allow that disparate data to be imported into a single table.

We have seen that SQL does have its limitations. Changing the structure of an existing table or maintaining an ID field can prove difficult and convoluted. It will sometimes prove necessary to operate *outside* of the database in order to make changes *inside*.

Database administrators are sometimes faced with sweeping reorganizations of existing databases. It may be decided that tables are to be combined, or that certain fields from certain tables are to be combined into new tables. The tables involved may contain thousands of records and the types of reconnections required may be beyond the means of SQL. It is in such a situation that the subtleties of the report writer might be enlisted to do what it was not intended to.

Since the report writer may select a record from one table, store the data locally, and then select from another table, it is ideally suited to gather bits and pieces from many tables into one newly restructured whole. This data can be written to a report suitable for import and then immediately imported into newly created tables within the database.

There is no danger in this procedure. The database may be reorganized without putting any data at risk. Data which is written to a report is *not* deleted from the database, or altered in any way. Similarly, imported data does not impact data already in the database. Only after the newly structured tables had been thoroughly tested would the old tables be deleted.

17. System Design

17.1   The Master Builder

Some, having mastered galliards and glissandos, entertain themselves and their friends. Others move on and write symphonies. The great bag of stuff that is a database implementation will not rehearse, nor will it perform, of its own accord. Nearly anyone could find, among it all, a melody to feel comfortable with, even to toy with, perhaps even teach to others. But to dare to pull it all together, to find *how* to rehearse it, and finally to conduct a successful and ongoing performance, is another matter.

Not only must the bits of the database itself, its entities and objects, the tables and views, establish orderly and rational links among themselves. Those entities and their linkings must then be gracefully integrated into the "add-ons," the applications such as forms and reports. And the applications must be constructed and orchestrated to find favor with that most difficult and demanding part of the system, the users.

Wonderfully experienced and sensitive managers have been placed in command of the motley crews who maintain our computers, and, knowing their users and knowing well what systems were needed, but not knowing the *how* of those systems, they failed. On the other hand, technical virtuosos have been given rein to realize their most clever and complex designs and have, in the end, engendered only user revolts and abandoned projects.

129

It isn't easy, bringing it all together. You must, all at once, build and learn and teach. You must be both coolly calculating and fast on your feet. You must, here, dare to experiment, and, there, demand that not the slightest risk be taken. The database administrator and designer must be both technician and diplomat to make the machinery kind to the people, and vice versa.

In this chapter we'll discuss some of the "larger issues" which crop up in relational database systems. A good designer will "see" these issues in every fragment of SQL syntax, and, equally, will "see" those fragments linked and supporting every issue.

17.2   The Primary Key

It has been stated repeatedly in this book that records within tables are *unordered*. The relational architecture takes its name from the notion of a *relation*. A relation is simply a table, which is simply a collection of records. Records are *related* in that they belong to the same table, the same relation. Records are *not* related in the sense that one is higher or lower than another, or that one comes first and another second, and so on. A record has no particular *place* in a table. This seeming chaos is at the very heart of the relational system, and is what allows it its great fluidity.

If a record has no place, no fixed residence, how then is it to be located? How is it to be distinguished from its neighbors? First, consider two records, which of course have the same fields (they would not be in the same table otherwise), and which have *exactly the same data* in their respective fields. How may we distinguish between these two records? We needn't try, for it is not possible. It is, unfortunately, in most relational database implementations, very possible to create two or more identical records. It is very important to note, however, that despite the fact that the two records, in their *physical* database presence, are separate and distinct, with regard to access to the database, they are *completely indistinguishable*. It is impossible to write a query that will select one and not the other. It is impossible to issue a delete command which will remove one and not the other.

TechNote: Some commercial implementations allow the selection, with any record of any table, of a field called something like ROWID. This field will contain a number which will be unique for that record within that table. The problem is that this number corresponds, more or less, to the *physical* location of the record on the computer's storage disk. All databases are, in one sense, entirely physical; they are bits of magnetic flux on a platter of metal oxide. But the databases that we have been discussing are in no way physical. They are *logical* constructs and their flexibility depends absolutely upon their remaining such. To build an application which must depend in any way upon a physical entity is a defeat. There's another small problem with ROWID: its value, for any given record, is not, nor can it be, permanent; it is subject to change.

The existence of records which cannot be distinguished is senseless. They are the same record. The storage of indistinguishable information is wonderfully useless. Our records must be stamped with uniqueness. Every record. We have bought uniqueness in some tables with the addition of an arbitrary number field, ID. Depending upon the nature of the data to be stored, this may be unnecessary. If personnel records included social security numbers, we could allow that field to provide our needed uniqueness.

Just as a bit of metal is the key which opens a door, just as the key to a puzzle is that which solves the mystery, so a unique field is the *key* to its record. The record cannot be retrieved without its key.

A key need not be a single field. A combination of fields may comprise a key to a record. If our personnel records contained separate fields for phone number and area code, neither one of those fields alone would guarantee uniqueness, but *combined* they would provide a key to all records (assuming that none of the people in our table were married to one another). Note carefully the following: No matter how many fields a record may contain, if a combination of any two of those fields is unique across the table, then the record containing those two fields is also unique. This is what we require of our keys, that they provide a unique identity to all of our records.

A record may have more than one key. Personnel records might contain an ID field as well as a Social Security number. Such records would have *three* keys: each of the two fields separately, and the two fields combined. A *primary key* is simply any field (or combination of fields) which identifies a record uniquely. Records may have more than one primary key. Records *must* have at least one primary key.

DesignNote: Since the full flexibility of the relational architecture depends upon the existence of primary keys, table design procedures should be developed that will insure that all new tables introduced into the database incorporate one or more fields which will comprise a primary key. Few if any commercial implementations provide any way of automatically enforcing the need for primary keys. The administrator may designate fields as being unique, or may create unique indexes. If the data which a proposed table is to hold does not lend itself to primary key creation, an arbitrarily numbered ID field could be added to the table definition. If data entry were done through the use of a forms application, an ID field could be maintained in a way which would be entirely transparent to the user.

17.3   Normalization

Normalization is a technical procedure which serves to optimize systems of tables within a relational database. It comes in many forms: first normal form, second normal form, third normal form, and so on. Most people avoid its complexities. So shall we, except to discuss what it in practice boils down to, a certain lack of redundancy. A man of some wisdom stated, in the 14th century, what has come to be known as *Ockham's Razor*: "Entities are not to be multiplied without necessity." The relational razor would bar the duplication of information.

Our personnel records must, of course, capture a person's address, including the name of the city in which the person resides. Fine, so we'll include in the record a text field of 30 or 40 characters and just write in the city names, such as "San Francisco." But what if we have 10, or 1,000, people who reside there? Are we to enter those same 13 characters 1,000 times? Should we consume our storage space with the repetition of identical pieces of information? And what if we have another table of, say, professional organizations? Are we to also duplicate those 13 characters for every organization in San Francisco?

The ultimate goal can easily be stated: Any given bit of information should exist, across the *entire database*, once and only once. This ultimate will never be reached, nor should it be. It would be possible to create a set of tables that would hold data on thousands of people without ever storing any given first name, such as "Mary," more than once, nor any last name more than once. Most would consider this taking normalization to abnormal extremes. William of Ockham did, after all, leave us some discretion, in the words "without necessity."

The rational and reasonable goal is to identify those pieces of information which will be required by records in multiple tables, to group that information into useful categories, and to place those groups in *their own tables*. City names, which we will want to incorporate in many different records in many different tables, should reside in a special table. So should state names. If we wished to capture the hobbies of our personnel, we would create a separate *hobbies* table, so that we should not have to store the string "skiing" many many times.

Having stored the string "San Francisco" once and only once, in its own *city* table, how is it to be made a part of many different records in many different tables? Through the use of *join columns*. Every record in the city table will be assigned a unique identifier, such as an id field, which will stand as the primary key of that record. We will deposit that primary key into a join column within our personnel record, and thus will someone be recorded as living in San Francisco.

Foreign keys

Just as a primary key is the key to its own table, the value in a join column is the key to *another* table. If we take the primary key value for the San Francisco record from the city table and deposit that value in the join column of a record in the personnel table, it remains a key. That value, within the personnel table, is not a primary key, for it does not refer to the personnel table (nor would it be unique within the personnel table). That value, when it has been placed within a personnel record, is a *foreign key*.

A foreign key is simply a primary key away from home. It is a primary key which has been copied *from* its own table *into* the join column of another table. It is the foreign keys which allow tables to be normalized. They provide the means of pointing to one item of information from many records in many tables. They provide links between data throughout the entire database.

> *DesignNote:* Since primary keys sally forth to become foreign keys and forge communications among the many tables of the database, these keys should be designed to be easily portable. If our personnel table contained a field for area code and another field for phone number, we might decide that the combination of these two fields would constitute the primary key for all personnel records (we would first have to decide not to hire married couples). This, however, would introduce a distinct design difficulty, for in order to use this primary key as a foreign key we would need to allocate *two* fields in the tables which were to receive the foreign key. When determining which data will constitute the primary key for a particular table, it is not sufficient to consider that table alone. Even the smallest design decisions should be viewed in terms of the entire database system.

One to One, One to Many

The problem which normalization addresses can be visualized if you remember that all links between data are two-way streets. When we record that Mary Moore lives in San Francisco, we are also saying that San Francisco holds a resident called Mary Moore. This may seem like the same thing stated with different words, but that is not the case. The two relationships are fundamentally different. There is a *structural* difference between these relationships that has profound consequences for database design.

The relationship between Mary Moore and her place of residence is *one to one*. She may reside in one and only one state (for tax purposes, at any rate). The relationship is the same as that between the name *Mary* and *Moore*. A first name can have only one last name associated with it.

— ONE TO ONE —

San Francisco   to   California

— ONE TO MANY —

California   to   San Francisco
                      Los Angeles
                      Sacramento
                      Fresno
                      Eureka
                      San Diego
                      :

Figure 17.1   One to one, one to many.

A one-to-one relationship can be captured in one database record. We can place first name, last name, and residence in a single record of our personnel table. We can do the same for any number of people. A *one-to-two* relationship can be captured in a single record. If nature had ordained that no human being will own more than two automobiles, we could allot within our personnel record two fields to hold two license plate numbers.

So long as we know beforehand, and know absolutely, that some *fixed* number is involved in the relationship, we can then go ahead and design a single record that will hold the data involved in that relationship. A *one-to-three* relationship could be captured, and so on. We might wind up with records containing a large and unwieldy number of fields, but so long as the numbers involved in the relationships are fixed for all time, it can be done.

What we cannot capture in a single record is a *one-to-many* relationship. We can record Mary and her place of residence, but suppose we wish to record that relationship in the other direction, San Francisco and its residents. We will design a record containing one field for city name and, well, how many fields shall we allot for names of residents? Let's be on the safe side, allow for expansion, and design the record with one million fields, one for city name and 999,999 for the names of residents. Apart from the fact that our database implementation probably won't allow this, we have a problem. What do we do when it comes time to enter *New York?*

A one-to-many relationship is simply one which is open-ended, one which has on the *many* side a number which cannot be known in advance. The number of cars which a person may own is in fact not limited. The relationship *car to owner* is one to one, but *owner to car* is one to many.

All of the above affects database design in a very straightforward fashion—the size of a record must be fixed at the moment of its creation, whereas the size of a table has no theoretical bound. A table *can* hold the residents of San Francisco. A table could hold the automobile registrations of the wealthiest person on the planet. If you look at Figure 17.1 you will see that the one-to-one relationship *resembles* a record; it's all nicely on one line. The one-to-many relationship, however, resembles no record ever seen.

Thus were born join columns and foreign keys. Our problem with San Francisco and New York is solved with but two tables. If we have a *city* table and a *people* table, we can simply take primary key values from the city table and drop them into the foreign key fields of the appropriate people records. We can record every resident of both cities, and we can, without any change to table or record structure, add Chicago, Miami, Denver...

> *TechNote:* In practice, even a *one-to-two* (and anything greater) relationship begs to be handled in multiple tables rather than multiple fields. There is nothing in the relational architecture which allows for searching fields *across* a single record. If we had a one million field record holding the population of San Francisco, how would we search for *Mary Moore?* The syntax does not provide for such things, and it never will.

> *DesignNote:* System design is not something apart from the real world. If you had never known a person to own more than a single automobile, you would not know to design a separate table for auto registrations. It is not enough to know every field that must be captured in the system of tables. You must know, *before* design can commence, the nature of the relationships that exist among those fields.

17.4   Referential Integrity

If yesterday Mary Moore moved to 132 Periwinkle Place, and today we look in the white pages and find that Mary Moore's address is 127 Periwinkle Place, what we have is a mistaken reference. The reference to Mary's address is wrong. The white pages is flawed; its *referential integrity* has been compromised. We could preserve the perfection of the white pages in one of two ways: 1, we could deny people the right to reside anywhere but at the address listed in the current white pages; 2, we could design a white pages which would update itself whenever anyone moved. The latter suggestion is perhaps the more practical, and would be quite feasible, were the white pages a relational database. At any rate, you can see the problem. When one thing refers to, or *points* to another thing, and that other thing moves (or disappears), the pointer is left askew.

Foreign keys are, of course, pointers. There is a pointer in Mary Moore's record which points to the city table, specifically to San Francisco. If, for whatever reason, San Francisco were removed from the city table, then the pointer in Mary Moore's record would point to... where? There are two possibilities. Remember that the foreign key in Mary's record is simply the value of San Francisco's primary key in the city table. In other words, it is probably some arbitrary number. If the San Francisco record is removed, along with its primary key, and if that key value is not assigned to another record in the city table, then Mary's pointer points to nowhere; it indicates a city which does not exist! If, after San Francisco is removed, its primary key value is assigned to the next city added to the database (say Dallas), then Mary's pointer will be pointing to the wrong city; it will indicate that Mary lives in Dallas!

The issue that referential integrity raises in the relational database world is one of enforcement: Should a database system enforce referential integrity, and if so, how? These questions await answers. Few, if any, commercial implementations offer procedures for ensuring referential integrity. Administrators and designers must use SQL and its applications to ensure whatever level of integrity they deem necessary.

In the example that we have been discussing, there is no question that referential integrity *should* be strictly enforced. The database system should be designed so that it is not possible for Mary Moore's personnel record to contain a foreign key which points to either a nonexistent city, or an incorrect one. How are such assurances to be implemented?

When the design procedure decides that two tables are to be linked, that the primary keys of one table will be used as foreign keys in the other table, that decision establishes a certain mutual dominion between the two tables. Record creation, alteration and deletion in one table should not take place without consulting the other table.

The procedures which are established for removing city names from the city table should mandate that the personnel table be consulted before deletion proceeds. If San Francisco is to be removed, and it is found that its primary key exists as a foreign key in the personnel table, then deletion should be disallowed. A record which is referenced from elsewhere in the database should not be removed. A correlated subquery could be used to discover if San Francisco's primary key was in use in the personnel table:

```
SELECT NAME FROM CITY X WHERE
((NAME = 'San Francisco') AND
EXISTS (SELECT * FROM PEOPLE
WHERE CITY = X.ID));
```

This query would return a record only if San Francisco was referenced in the personnel table.

Whenever a record is added to the personnel table, the foreign key value placed in its city field should be taken directly from the city table. Data entry staff should not be allowed to enter foreign key values. Rather, a forms application should be devised which allows them to enter "San Francisco," and which then queries the city table and places the appropriate value into the new personnel record. The database design should strive to make table linkings and the exchange of key values invisible to the user. As much as is possible, all such links should be forged automatically by the application programs.

Procedures should be developed to confirm referential integrity across the database and should be executed on a regular basis. The following query will return the name of anyone in the personnel table whose record contains a reference to a city which does not exist in the city table:

```
SELECT FNAME, LNAME FROM PEOPLE X WHERE
NOT EXISTS (SELECT * FROM CITY
WHERE ID = X.CITY);
```

Similar queries could be developed to confirm the integrity of all table-to-table links. Note that the above query will *not* reveal if Mary Moore's record points to the *wrong* city. *Nonexistent* links can be ferreted out at any time. *Incorrect* links must be precluded at data entry.

17.5   A Table With No Data

Imagine, if you will, a group of people, individuals from all over the country, who have formed a school, an informal school wherein they will teach one another. Each will teach some skill or bit of knowledge to the others. The classes will be held hither and yon, wherever in the country is convenient for both teacher and students. Anyone can teach any course. Anyone can attend any course. The school keeps track of its comings and goings in a relational database. Its courses are listed in the table COURSES. Students and teachers are held in the PEOPLE table. Possible locations for courses are listed in the CITY table. The school has only one department, named, for no good reason, the "Advertising Department," and its expenditures are tracked in a table called ADVERT. (The school has kindly allowed these tables to be reproduced in Appendix A.)

Thinking all of this a rather good idea, and thinking that this good idea might catch on, the founders of this school designed their tables to allow

COURSE	TEACHER	STUDENT	LOCATION
12	6		11
12		3	11
12		7	11
12		1	11
12		12	11
1		3	27
1		9	27
4	11		4
1	1		27
4		9	4
4		1	4
1		12	4
1		13	4
1		14	4
7		14	8
10		13	15
7	9		8
7	13		8
11		9	21
11		8	21
10		7	15
11		2	21
10		1	15
11	4		21
10	8		15
⋮	⋮	⋮	⋮

Figure 17.2   The school table.

for expansion. The PEOPLE table could go on and on, registering teachers and students without end. The COURSES table could hold as many courses as there were course names. Every city in the country could be listed in the CITY table, if need be. They now needed some sort of master table that would allow them to enroll any number of students in a wide variety of courses located heaven knows where.

They devised the SCHOOL table, which proved not quite adequate, since, among other things, it couldn't tell them *when* courses would be held. But it was a good start. The essence of the table is that it contains *no data whatsoever!* It may seem as though it contains data (see Figure 17.2), but don't be fooled; all those numbers are not data. They are not useful bits of information taken from the world at large and stored for later perusal. The numbers, every last one of them, were generated internally, within the database, and are, in a way, entirely random. All of the numbers are *foreign keys*. Every field in every record of the SCHOOL table is a pointer which refers to some bit of data stored elsewhere in the database.

To judge the cleverness of their creation, let us consider a typical record:

COURSE	TEACHER	STUDENT	LOCATION
4		9	4

The first thing we note is that this is a "student" record, for the TEACHER field is null. The first number in the record, 4, is the primary key value of a record in the COURSES table, in this case the course "Modern Dance." The second number, 9, identifies the student by pointing to a record in the PEOPLE table, here indicating "Connie DeMarco." The third number, 4, duplicates the primary key of "Portland" in the CITY table. We could find the "teacher" record (or records) for this course with the following query:

SELECT * FROM SCHOOL WHERE
TEACHER IS NOT NULL
AND COURSE =
(SELECT ID FROM COURSES WHERE
NAME = 'Modern Dance');

Our inquiry would deliver the following record:

COURSE	TEACHER	STUDENT	LOCATION
4	11		4

Here the second number, 11, points to the "Mary Bennett" record in the PEOPLE table. Mary is a dancer and the teacher of this course. Note that we might have found multiple "teacher" records for this course. This is the beauty of the table. A course might have more than one teacher. Well, the table can accommodate multiple "teacher" records for any particular course, just as it accommodates multiple "student" records for every course.

If you look carefully at the individual records above and at the table in Figure 17.2, and if you study the structures of the various tables whose

```
SELECT FNAME, LNAME FROM PEOPLE WHERE ID IN
(SELECT STUDENT FROM SCHOOL WHERE
COURSE = (SELECT ID FROM COURSES WHERE
NAME = 'Performing Shakespeare'));
```

FNAME	LNAME
Jonathan	Drake
David	Dryden
Jennifer	Mallory
Martha	Redwood

Figure 17.3   Students in the Shakespeare course.

---

primary keys went to fill the SCHOOL table, you will find that any number
of different courses could be accommodated. Any course could have any
number of students. Any course could have any number of teachers. The
table will even allow one person to register as both student and teacher for
the same course (student, perhaps, while a co-teacher conducts her part of
the course).

Once the SCHOOL table has been designed, and the forms applications
are in place for data entry, and the reports applications have been written
to print the rosters of each course, no one need ever see any of the numbers
which actually comprise the table. The numbers, the pointers, the foreign
keys, should remain at all times "in the background," doing their work
unseen. The names associated with the SCHOOL table, the names of courses,
teachers, students, and locations, can all be found without knowing any of
the foreign key numbers. Through the "switchyard" of the SCHOOL table,
names can be found using other names (see Figure 17.3). A table with no
data can, invisibly, lead the user to many tables filled with much data.

The tables in this book are unusual only in their size. Tables in working database implementations will comprise thousands, perhaps millions, of
records. Given a computer large enough, with storage disks large enough,
and a SQL implementation of sufficient power, the SCHOOL table and its at-
tendant tables could list every course taught in every school in this country,
along with every teacher and all of the millions of students.

18. Programming with SQL

He who tells a secret is another's servant.

GRANT SELECT ON HOW TO PUBLIC;

18.1   The Cognoscenti

The programmer is sometimes seen as the high priest of the computer installation, performing mysterious and inexplicable exercises which often result in miraculous cures, and sometimes result in catastrophic maladies. She speaks an arcane tongue and writes languages which seem nothing less than hieroglyphics. Programming with SQL changes none of that. It does not cause a change in the language which the programmer uses, nor does it cause changes in any of the procedures. SQL brings an *addition* to the progamming language, an addition with which we have become very familiar, and this added portion of the language will be written, for the most part, in a way with which we are equally familiar. What SQL adds to programming languages is, simply, SQL; it adds SELECT, UPDATE, INSERT, and other SQL statements which are written in exactly the same way they are in interactive SQL. You could scan through programs written in ADA, or BASIC, or C, or COBOL, and find SELECT statements written just as they have been throughout this book.

SQL is *embedded* in the programmer's language; SQL statements are simply written into the program at whatever point they are needed. The data retrieved is deposited into the program's variables and is then acted upon just as any program data would be. In like manner, an embedded

DML statement would move data from the program's variables to the database. The programmer who would use SQL must in effect write two languages simultaneously, switching back and forth depending upon whether the database is being accessed or local variables are being manipulated. Use of the one language in no way affects the syntax of the other.

The examples in this book will use the 'C' programming language. The embedded SQL statements, should, however, appear the same in whatever language is being used.

18.2   The Precompiler

A relational database implementation which allows access to the database through a programming language (not all do) will provide, as part of its "package," a *precompiler*. The compiler used by the programmer will, of course, not recognize SQL statements. Nor will it have any knowledge of the database. The precompiler is simply a utility which reads the programmer's code and converts all SQL statements into "host" code. The resulting code will contain only statements which are legal in the language being used. The program can now be compiled successfully. The program will gain knowledge of the database by being "linked" to code, provided by the database vendor, which contains this knowledge.

All SQL statements embedded in a host language program will begin with the words EXEC SQL. These words serve to alert the precompiler to the presence of statements which need translating into the host language. SQL statements will terminate with a semicolon when embedded in the 'C' language. The end-of-line character will vary with the host language and the database implementation.

18.3   Variables

Any host variable which will be referred to in a SQL statement must be declared in a section which opens with the line:

EXEC SQL BEGIN DECLARE SECTION;

and ends with the line:

EXEC SQL END DECLARE SECTION;

See Figure 18.1. No variable may be used in a SQL statement unless it has first been declared. The *type* of variable which may be declared is limited. Arrays and structures are disallowed. Host variables may have the same names as table fields. Host variables, when used in SQL statements, are always prefaced with a colon (*:variable*). This serves to distinguish them from field names. When *outside* SQL statements, host variables are, of course, used normally, without the colon.

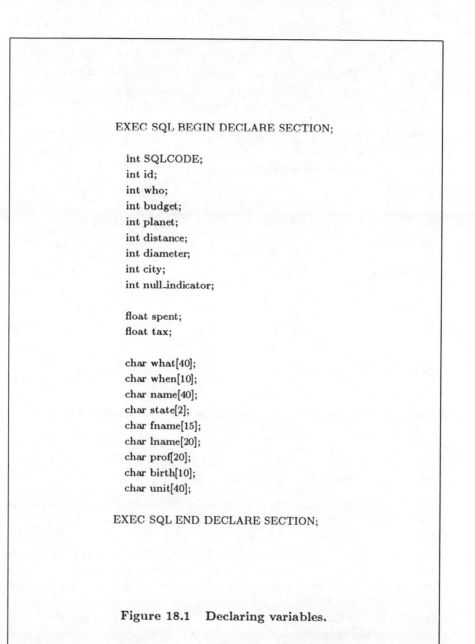

```
EXEC SQL BEGIN DECLARE SECTION;

    int SQLCODE;
    int id;
    int who;
    int budget;
    int planet;
    int distance;
    int diameter;
    int city;
    int null_indicator;

    float spent;
    float tax;

    char what[40];
    char when[10];
    char name[40];
    char state[2];
    char fname[15];
    char lname[20];
    char prof[20];
    char birth[10];
    char unit[40];

EXEC SQL END DECLARE SECTION;
```

Figure 18.1   Declaring variables.

⋮

```
EXEC SQL WHENEVER NOT FOUND CONTINUE;
EXEC SQL WHENEVER SQLERROR CONTINUE;
EXEC SQL DECLARE C1 CURSOR FOR
    SELECT NAME, DISTANCE FROM S_SYSTEM
        WHERE DIATANCE <> 0;

EXEC SQL OPEN C1;

EXEC SQL FETCH C1 INTO
    :name, :distance;

if (SQLCODE == 100)
    do_not_found();

if (SQLCODE < 0)
    do_error();

EXEC SQL CLOSE C1;
```

⋮

Figure 18.2   Branching on SQLCODE.

Error Indicator

A special host variable, SQLCODE, must be declared. This variable will be filled whenever a SQL statement is executed, and its value will indicate the success or failure of the statement. The values returned in this variable will vary with the database implementation. The ANSI standard mentions only two values, 100 and "a negative number." A negative number returned in SQLCODE indicates that the statement did not execute, that some error occurred. A negative number would be returned if the syntax of the statement were incorrect, or if a nonexistent field name were used. The value 100 indicates that no record was found. This value would be returned on the very first execution of a SELECT statement, indicating that *no* records met the query conditions, or it might be returned on subsequent executions, indicating that the *last* record meeting the query conditions had been found.

$\vdots$

```
EXEC SQL WHENEVER NOT FOUND GOTO handle_not_found;
EXEC SQL WHENEVER SQLERROR GOTO handle_error;
EXEC SQL DECLARE C1 CURSOR FOR
  SELECT NAME, DISTANCE FROM S SYSTEM
    WHERE DIATANCE <> 0;

EXEC SQL OPEN C1

EXEC SQL FETCH C1 INTO
  :name, :distance;

EXEX SQL CLOSE C1;
```

$\vdots$

Figure 18.3   Branching with WHENEVER.

18.4   Branching

Embedded SQL provides two branching instructions, allowing the program to test for "error" or "not found" and to jump to routines designed to handle these conditions. The syntax for these statements is:

EXEC SQL WHENEVER NOT FOUND GOTO label;

EXEC SQL WHENEVER SQLERROR GOTO label;

These statements may be written at any point in the program. Once a label is associated with an error condition it remains in effect for the remainder of the program, unless another WHENEVER statement is used to change it. The WHENEVER conditions may be cancelled with the word CONTINUE:

EXEC SQL WHENEVER NOT FOUND CONTINUE;

EXEC SQL WHENEVER SQLERROR CONTINUE;

If a CONTINUE statement has been executed, for the remainder of the program, or until another WHENEVER statement is encountered, no action will be taken for that particular error condition.

The WHENEVER statements simply direct the precompiler to insert an "if SQLCODE...goto label" after every occurrence of a SQL statement. The programmer may code such statements directly, and more flexibly, without using the WHENEVER statements (see Figure 18.2). If SQLCODE is to be checked directly by the program, CONTINUE statements should be used to

⋮

```
        EXEC SQL DECLARE C1 CURSOR FOR
          SELECT FNAME, LNAME FROM PEOPLE
          WHERE LNAME > 'S';

        EXEC SQL OPEN C1;

        while (TRUE)
          {
          EXEC SQL FETCH C1 INTO
            :fname, :lname;
          if (SQLCODE == 100)
            break;
          if (SQLCODE < 0)
            break;
          if strcmp(lname, "Stevens")
            break;
          }

        EXEX SQL CLOSE C1;
```

⋮

Figure 18.4   Fetching repeatedly.

---

prevent the precompiler from inserting its own branching code.

18.5   The Cursor

In order to execute a query within a program we must first *declare* the SQL statement which is to be used in that query. When a statement is declared, an area is set aside within the program to hold the results of the query. This area is known as a *cursor*. When a SQL statement is declared, a cursor name must also be declared and associated with that particular statement:

        EXEC SQL DECLARE C1 CURSOR FOR SELECT ... ;

Once a cursor has been declared, the query may be executed by first performing an *open* on the cursor, and then performing one or more *fetches*:

        EXEC SQL OPEN C1;

⋮

```
EXEC SQL DECLARE C1 CURSOR FOR
    SELECT ID FROM S_SYSTEM
        WHERE NAME = :name;

EXEC SQL DECLARE C2 CURSOR FOR
    SELECT NAME, DISTANCE, DIAMETER
    FROM MOONS
        WHERE PLANET = :id;

EXEC SQL OPEN C1;

EXEC SQL OPEN C2;

strcpy(name, "Jupiter");

EXEC SQL FETCH C1 INTO
    :id;

EXEC SQL FETCH C2 INTO
    :name, :distance, :diameter;

EXEX SQL CLOSE C1;

EXEX SQL CLOSE C2;
```

⋮

Figure 18.5   One query feeds another.

EXEC SQL FETCH C1 INTO :var1, :var2;

When no more data is required, or when the last row has been found, a *close* is performed on the cursor:

EXEC SQL CLOSE C1;

See Figure 18.4 for an example of how these statements might appear as a portion of an actual program.

One Row at a Time

In embedded SQL, a FETCH command retrieves only a single row at a time. The OPEN command "primes" the query, so that the first fetch performed after the open will collect the first row that meets the query's conditions. Subsequent fetches retrieve any additional rows which satisfy the query, one at a time. If fetches are executed after receiving an error or a "not found," those fetches will simply continue to receive the same failure message, over and over. The query can be repeated, "top to bottom," only by closing the cursor, reopening it, and *then* fetching.

The conditions in WHERE clauses may reference program variables (see figure 18.5). This means, in part, that a query could be opened at the start of a program and held open. The program could select needed records by changing the values in the variables referenced in the WHERE clause. A cursor may be held open for the duration of the program, and need be closed only when the program exits.

The limit to the number of cursors that may be opened simultaneously will be imposed by the particular database implementation, and will probably be related to the availability of system memory. The limit *should* be some healthy number. With numerous cursors held open, values retrieved from one query can immediately be used to "feed" other queries.

18.6　Selecting Single Rows

If it is known that a query will return only a single record, the SELECT statement may be embedded without the use of a cursor. The statement must be preceded by the words EXEC SQL. The local variables which will receive the selected data are indicated just as they are in a FETCH statement:

EXEC SQL SELECT ID
INTO :id FROM TABLES
WHERE NAME = :name;

If no rows are found which meet the apecified conditions, SQLCODE will be set to 100 (not found). If a non-cursor embedded select statement returns more than a single row, SQLCODE will be set to a negative value (indicating an error).

⋮

```
EXEC SQL SELECT ID
   INTO :id INDICATOR :null_indicator
   FROM TABLES
      WHERE NAME = :name;

If (SQLCODE __ 100)
   do_not_found();

if (SQLCODE < 0)
   do_error();

if (null_indicator < 0)
   do_got_null();
```

⋮

Figure 18.6   Using the null indicator.

Null Indicator

Can embedded SQL queries retrieve null values? Not directly, of course, for null is no value at all and therefore can not very well be placed into a variable. The *presence* of a null may be determined using an *indicator*. An indicator is simply a host variable which is specified in the query, along with the variable which is to receive the retrieved data. The name of the indicator follows the data variable name, and is separated from it by the word INDICATOR:

```
EXEC SQL SELECT ID
INTO :id INDICATOR :null_indicator
FROM TABLES WHERE NAME = :name;
```

After the query has completed, if a null was returned for the data variable, the indicator variable will be set to a negative value. A non-negative value in the indicator variable indicates that a non-null value was returned to the data variable. See Figure 18.6. Regardless of what may be returned in the null indicator, SQLCODE should be examined to determine the status of the query.

```
EXEC SQL INSERT
INTO TABLES (ID, NAME)
VALUES (:id, :name);

EXEC SQL UPDATE TABLES
SET NAME = :name
WHERE ID = :id;

EXEC SQL DELETE
FROM TABLES
WHERE NAME = :name;
```

Figure 18.7   Embedded DML verbs.

18.7   Insert, Update, Delete

The DML verbs, INSERT, UPDATE, and DELETE may be embedded in host programs just as the single row SELECT is, by prefacing the statements with the words EXEC SQL. The syntax of the statements are no different from those in interactive SQL. Host variables are referred to, as always, by adding a colon. See Figure 18.7 for examples of embedded DML syntax.

18.8   Dynamic SQL

Some commercial implementations of embedded SQL allow for the preparation and execution of *dynamic* statements. These are statements which are either entered into the program by a user, or statements which the program itself composes. The point of dynamic SQL is that *any* query which can be imagined can be executed. The query need not have been composed by the programmer when she was writing the program. A program written last year might, for example, read a file written last week and execute any query listed in that file. Typically, the statement is composed in a buffer, and is then *prepared*:

EXEC SQL PREPARE S FROM :buffer;

What must, or can be done with the prepared statement will vary with the implementation. The best of them allow for any number of fields to be selected and for the FETCH to be performed without the specification of particular variables for the reception of data. In such a case, the statement returns a pointer to an array and a count of the array elements. The program then transfers the array data to its own variables.

18.9   The Power of the Thing

The power and flexibility that embedded SQL gives to a host language should be recognized. The database is accessible in ways undreamed of by interactive users. Even the most sophisticated of forms applications or report generators will be be unable to approximate what may be done with embedded SQL. The programmer can not only reach all parts of the database, she can reach all parts *simultaneously*, doing what she will when she will.

Appendix A: The Tables

Tables are listed alphabetically by table name.

CREATE TABLE ADVERT
(WHO NUMBER, WHEN DATE, WHAT CHAR(40), BUDGET NUMBER,
SPENT NUMBER, TAX NUMBER);

WHO	WHEN	WHAT	BUDGET	SPENT	TAX
1	31-DEC-86	New Year's Party	200	212.34	11.87
7	05-JAN-87	Catalog	350	327.65	19.66
	10-JAN-87	Postage		44.65	0.00
	11-JAN-87	Telephone	100	101.77	6.06
13	15-JAN-87	Travel - Atlanta	500	443.09	31.00
8	21-JAN-87	Dinner for 4		106.73	6.40
6	29-JAN-87	Lunch for 3		52.88	3.17

```
CREATE TABLE CITY
(ID NUMBER, NAME CHAR(40), STATE CHAR(2));
```

ID	NAME	STATE
1	New York	NY
2	San Francisco	CA
3	Chicago	IL
4	Portland	OR
5	Durham	NC
6	Miami	FL
7	Atlanta	GA
8	Boise	ID
9	Santa Fe	NM
10	Lexington	KY
11	Flagstaff	AZ
12	Carson City	NV
13	Lansing	MI
14	Denver	CO
15	Honolulu	HI
16	Spokane	WA
17	Bismarck	ND
18	Portsmouth	NH
19	Providence	RI
20	Albany	NY
21	Seattle	WA
22	Moscow	ID
23	Tucson	AZ
24	Macon	GA
25	Buffalo	NY
26	San Jose	CA
27	Tampa	FL

```
CREATE TABLE COURSES
(ID NUMBER, NAME CHAR(40));
```

ID	NAME
1	Introduction to law
2	Human anatomy
3	Basic baking
4	Modern Dance
5	Household accounting
6	Appreciating ballet
7	Portfolio management
8	Caring for common ailments
9	Beginning flute
10	Introduction to BASIC
11	Getting your flying license
12	Performing Shakespeare
13	Caring for common ailments

CREATE TABLE DUMMY (ID NUMBER);

$$\frac{\text{ID}}{0}$$

```
CREATE TABLE MONTH
(SUN NUMBER(2), MON NUMBER(2),
TUE NUMBER(2), WED NUMBER(2),
THU NUMBER(2), FRI NUMBER(2), SAT NUMBER(2));
```

SUN	MON	TUE	WED	THU	FRI	SAT
1	2	3	4	5	6	7
8	9	10	11	12	13	14
15	16	17	18	19	20	21
22	23	24	25	26	27	28
29	30	31				

```
CREATE TABLE MOONS
(PLANET NUMBER, NAME CHAR(30),
DISTANCE NUMBER, DIAMETER NUMBER);
```

PLANET	NAME	DISTANCE	DIAMETER
3	Moon	384000	3480
4	Phobos	9354	27
4	Deimos	23490	15
5	Io	422000	3632
5	Europa	671000	3126
5	Ganymede	1070000	5276
5	Callisto	1880000	4820
6	Mimas	186000	392
6	Enceladus	238000	510
6	Tethys	295000	1060
6	Dione	377000	1120
6	Rhea	527000	1530
6	Titan	1222000	5150
6	Hyperion	1481000	205
6	Iapetus	3561000	1460
6	Phoebe	12954000	220
7	Miranda	130000	320
7	Ariel	192000	1300
7	Umbriel	267000	1100
7	Titania	438000	1600
7	Oberon	586000	1620
8	Triton	355000	4000
8	Nereid	5562000	500
9	Charon	17000	1200

CREATE TABLE PEOPLE
(ID NUMBER, FNAME CHAR(15), LNAME CHAR(20), PROF CHAR(20),
BIRTH DATE, CITY NUMBER, STATE CHAR(2));

ID	FNAME	LNAME	PROF	BIRTH	CITY	STATE
1	Jennifer	Mallory	Lawyer	10-APR-47	1	NY
2	Margaret	Langer	Doctor	09-JUN-50	2	CA
3	Jonathan	Drake	Cook	20-SEP-60	3	IL
4	David	Braverman	Pilot	12-MAY-57	10	KY
5	Daisy	Escher	Dentist	05-AUG-59	13	MI
6	Mary	DeMott	Actress	23-DEC-58	11	AZ
7	David	Dryden	Musician	03-FEB-49	14	CO
8	Elizabeth	Floyd	Programmer	05-SEP-57	6	FL
9	Connie	DeMarco	Broker	09-MAY-54	3	IL
10	Mark	Feldman	Doctor	04-FEB-57	11	AZ
11	Mary	Bennett	Dancer	21-OCT-55	6	FL
12	Martha	Redwood	Accountant	23-MAY-56	10	KY
13	Lance	Roberts	Dancer	11-JUL-50	11	AZ

```
CREATE TABLE S_SYSTEM
(ID NUMBER, NAME CHAR(20),
DISTANCE NUMBER, DIAMETER NUMBER);
```

ID	NAME	DISTANCE	DIAMETER
0	Sun	0	865400
1	Mercury	36	3100
2	Venus	67	7700
3	Earth	93	7927
4	Mars	141	4200
5	Jupiter	483	88700
6	Saturn	887	75100
7	Uranus	1783	32000
8	Neptune	2795	27700
9	Pluto	3675	1500

CREATE TABLE SCHOOL
(COURSE NUMBER, TEACHER NUMBER,
STUDENT NUMBER, LOCATION NUMBER);

COURSE	TEACHER	STUDENT	LOCATION
12	6		11
12		3	11
12		7	11
12		1	11
12		12	11
1		3	27
1		9	27
4	11		4
1	1		27
4		9	4
4		1	4
1		12	4
1		13	4
1		14	4
7		14	8
10		13	15
7	9		8
7	13		8
11		9	21
11		8	21
10		7	15
11		2	21
10		1	15
11	4		21
10	8		15

```
CREATE TABLE STATE
(NAME CHAR(40), STATE CHAR(2));
```

NAME	STATE
Alaska	AL
Arizona	AZ
California	CA
Colorado	CO
Dist. of Columbia	DC
Florida	FL
Georgia	GA
Hawaii	HI
Idaho	ID
Illinois	IL
Kentucky	KY
Massachusetts	MA
Michigan	MI
Nevada	NV
New Hampshire	NH
New Mexico	NM
New York	NY
North Carolina	NC
North Dakota	ND
Oregon	OR
Rhode Island	RI
Utah	UT
Washington	WA

```
CREATE TABLE TABLES
(ID NUMBER, NAME CHAR(30));
```

ID	NAME
1	MONTH
2	S_SYSTEM
3	PEOPLE
4	MOONS
5	UNITS
6	CITY
7	STATE
8	ADVERT

```
CREATE TABLE UNITS
(TID NUMBER, FNAME CHAR(30), UNIT CHAR(40));
```

TID	FNAME	UNIT
1	DISTANCE	Millions of miles from Sun
1	DIAMETER	Miles
4	DIAMETER	Kilometers
4	DISTANCE	Kilometers from planet
8	BUDGET	Dollars
8	SPENT	Dollars
8	TAX	Dollars

Appendix B: Reserved Words

The following are the words listed in the ANSI standard as belonging to the language:

ALL	AND	ANY
AS	ASC	AUTHORIZATION
AVG	BEGIN	BETWEEN
BY	CHAR	CHARACTER
CHECK	CLOSE	COBOL
COMMIT	CONTINUE	COUNT
CREATE	CURRENT	CURSOR
DEC	DECIMAL	DECLARE
DELETE	DESC	DISTINCT
DOUBLE	END	ESCAPE
EXEC	EXISTS	FETCH
FLOAT	FOR	FORTRAN
FOUND	FROM	GO
GOTO	GRANT	GROUP
HAVING	IN	INDICATOR
INSERT	INT	INTEGER
INTO	IS	LANGUAGE
LIKE	MAX	MIN
MODULE	NOT	NULL
NUMERIC	OF	ON
OPEN	OPTION	OR
ORDER	PASCAL	PLI
PRECISION	PRIVILEGES	PROCEDURE
PUBLIC	REAL	ROLLBACK
SCHEMA	SECTION	SELECT
SET	SMALLINT	SOME
SQL	SQLCODE	SQLERROR
SUM	TABLE	TO
UNION	UNIQUE	UPDATE
USER	VALUES	VIEW
WHENEVER	WHERE	WITH
WORK		

Every programming language has reserved words and SQL is no exception. The words above have been "reserved" for those who would implement a SQL database. They have been held aside for use by SQL. You, the user of SQL, may *not* use these words as *names*. You, of course, can, and must, use the above words in order to use SQL, but you may not use any of the words as either a table name or a field name. Were you to attempt to name a field "field," you would be presented with the error message "Invalid column name," or some such. It is possible that particular implementations will not reserve all of the words above, and that it may reserve words not listed above. Since the above words have received the ANSI imprimatur, it is best to avoid them even if your implementation does not insist.

Appendix C: Glossary

alias   Some word which is used to stand for a TABLE name within a select statement.

ANSI   American National Standards Institute, 1430 Broadway, New York, NY 10018. ANSI establishes voluntary technical standards for both hardware and software.

application   A computer program which does some bit of useful work, or a file containing a set of instructions for the computer.

ASCII   Pronounced "AS-key," a method of encoding characters within a computer. ASCII is used in *all* personal computers and in all mini- and mainframe computers *except* those manufactured by IBM.

attribute   In formal relational terminology, a FIELD, or COLUMN, is known as an attribute.

authorization identifier   A name, usually the user's login name, which is assigned as part of the full name for any table or view created by the user.

base table   A "real" table, one which contains data and occupies space within the database. It is from BASE tables that VIRTUAL tables are built.

catalog   The collection of SYSTEM TABLES which are created by the database system itself, and which it uses to maintain tables and views created by users.

column   The vertical component of the TABLE structure. A column will be comprised of one or more FIELDS, each of the same DATA TYPE.

correlation name   A table name ALIAS, in the ANSI standard, is referred to as a "correlation name."

concatenation   The combining of two or more character strings into a single string.

CREATE   The DDL verb used to bring into being new database objects, such as tables and views.

data   Information, whether numeric or textual, which has been broken into pieces which conform to certain structure types, such as INTEGER, STRING, DECIMAL, etc.

database   A collection of DATA which provides for rapid and varied paths of access.

database administrator   Someone appointed to look after the database. This person will determine who will be allowed to view and/or update the tables in the database.

data entry   The process of populating the database, of creating the myriad number of records which comprise a functioning database. This is the province of the DML verbs.

data type   A FIELD, the smallest structure within a relational database, cannot be created until it has been declared to be of some particular pre-defined *type*, such as *numeric, date,* or *character.* A field cannot be disassociated from its type.

DCL   Data Control Language.   The verbs used to create and remove database privileges.

DDL   Data Definition Language.   The verbs used to create and remove database objects, such as tables and views.

DELETE   The DML verb used to remove records from tables.

DML   Data Manipulation Language.   The verbs used to add and alter records within tables.

DROP   Although not included in the ANSI standard, this is the accepted DML verb for deleting tables and views.

EBCDIC   Pronounced "EBB-si-dik," a method of encoding characters within a computer. EBCDIC is used in mainframe computers manufactured by IBM.

embedded SQL   SQL statements used within a "host" programming language.

error message   This is what you will receive, instead of data, if your SQL statement is incorrectly worded. An error message *should* include information telling you *why* your statement has been rejected.

escape character   Any character which has a special, "command" meaning to the database system (or within a forms or report application).   The name is taken from the ASCII escape character, which is traditionally used as a command character but is unprintable.

field   The smallest of the structures comprising the relational architecture, a field will hold one piece of data and will have a structure corresponding to the data type.

flow control   In a report application or program, the statements which determine what lines are to be executed next.

form   A formatted and labeled collection of data which is written upon a computer terminal. Forms are usually "interactive," allowing a user to change data or add new data to the database *through* the form.

full field name   A compound name which includes both a table name and a field name, and which uniquely identifies a field across the entire database.

full table name   A compound name which includes both an authorization identifier and a table name, and which uniquely identifies a table in a multi-user relational database system.

GRANT   A DCL verb, used to bestow privileges upon other users.

index   A structure external to a relation, which gives to that relation (or TABLE), something which it by definition cannot possess intrinsically, *order*. A collection of *pointers*, a map, which, if followed, leads from row to row within a table, not as those rows actually reside, but as they *would* reside, were they *ordered*.

INSERT   A DML verb, used to add new records to a table.

interactive   A mode of computer operation in which a person enters commands at a keyboard and the computer responds through the display terminal.

join column   A column whose values may be used to connect the records of one table to those of another table. The record in table *A* will have in its join column the same value as that in the join column of the record in table *B*.

label   A name whcich marks a particular line in a report application or a program.

operator   A statement which performs some operation upon a piece of data.

portable   An adjective denoting procedures developed at one database implemention which could easily be moved, or "ported to," and used at another site.

query language   A limited collection of words, and a strictly defined syntax, which are used to probe the information contained within a database.

record   A ROW, the horizontal component of a TABLE.

relation   In formal terminology, a TABLE is known as a relation. A relation is similar to the mathematical notion of a *set*, or a collection, in this case a collection of rows. The rows within a relation are *unordered*.

relational database   A database which consists of a collection of tables.

reserved word A word which is a part of a programming or query language and which may be used only as the language prescribes. Specifically, reserved words may not be used as names of objects.

REVOKE Although not included in the ANSI standard, this is the accepted DCL verb for removing privileges.

row Also known as a RECORD, a ROW is the horizontal component of a TABLE structure. A row will be comprised of one or more fields. The fields comprising a row may be of identical or of different data types.

schema A portion of a multi-user database which belongs to a single user, comprising all tables and views created by that user.

SELECT The SQL workhorse, the query verb which runs and fetches.

site-specific An adjective denoting tables or procedures which are specific to a particular database implementation, and which may or may not be "portable" to other implementations.

string A group of characters (letters, numbers, punctuation, spaces) taken as a whole. A string of characters. The word "string" is a string, as is "the string," "233," "234 Maple Lane," etc.

structured An application or program which is divided by function into easily understood, logically contained, sections is said to be *structured*.

system tables Tables created and maintained by the database system itself, containing information about the system, such as table and field names.

table The basic structure in the relational database architecture, it is itself composed of records and fields, rows and columns. In the formal terminology, a table is known as a RELATION.

tuple In formal relational terminology, a ROW is known as a TUPLE. Webster defines a TUPLE as a "set of elements, usually a set with ordered elements."

UPDATE A DML verb, used to change data within existing records.

variable A data storage area created within a forms application, a report application, or a program. Having a definite data type, it is very much like a table FIELD, but is independent of other variables.

VIEW A virtual table.

virtual Something which exists logically, but which has no independent physical existence. Computer operating systems, through the clever manipulation of storage devices, can provide to users a virtual memory which may be many times larger than the physical memory installed in the machine.

virtual table   A VIEW, a table which consists of nothing more than a definition, and which itself contains no data. The definition will point to bits and pieces of BASE tables, whose data will *appear* to belong to the virtual table.

Appendix D: Chronology

Developments and announcements concerning SQL following the adoption by ANSI as a standard:

12/7/87   "**Informix-SQL** from **Informix Software Inc.** is a low-cost, full-featured SQL-based relational database management system that has long had a strong following in the **Unix** market. Now that Informix-SQL is available across the three most common hardware platforms—midrange computers, mainframe computers, and microcomputers—and can be run under the most widely used operating systems—**VMS** on VAXes, **MVS** on IBM mainframes, and **DOS** on IBM-PCs and compatibles—it is growing even more in popularity." Betty Y. Forman and Jack Fegreus, *Digital Review.*

12/7/87   "Microcomputer database maker **Microrim Inc.** last week announced new versions of its **R:Base** system for **OS/2** and **DOS** environments, as well as a new configuration of the database management system (DBMS) for local area networks. The new products feature embedded Structured Query Language (SQL) commands, improved ease of use features and much faster operation..." Patricia Zengerle, *MIS Week.*

12/7/87   "**Ashton-Tate Corp.**'s super-secret **dBase IV**...slated for first-quarter 1988, is an almost total rewrite of **dBase III Plus**, released in 1985. In a major about-face, the new package supports a full structured-query-language (SQL) database interface, compatible with the mainframe standard set by **IBM**." Ray Weiss, *Electronic Engineering Times.*

12/7/87   "After being turned down by two industry sponsors, the **Dbase** standards committee last week said it will seek the support of the IEEE in defining a standard for the Dbase language...ANSI rejected the group's appeal to sponsor a standard, saying that the SQL standard was a preexisting, conflicting standard." Rachel Parker, *Info World.*

11/24/87   "**Ashton-Tate** is building everything but the kitchen sink into the next release of **dBASE** to keep its customer base from going down the drain...Along with a revamped engine to boost performance and Structured Query Language (SQL) commands embedded in the dBASE language, the next release of dBASE will incorporate a template language, a macro language..." Beth Freedman, *PC Week.*

11/23/87   "**Dataease** said it will support Structured Query Language (SQL), the emerging standard to store and retrieve information in relational databases, and position its flagship product **Dataease** as the applications development front end to SQL engines of all types." Scott Mace, *Info World*.

11/23/87   "**Information Builders Inc.** (**IBI**) has released version 1.1 of **Focus** for **Unix**, including **VAX/Ultrix** systems...The new Focus includes an SQL parser for querying Focus database files, enhancements for accessing remote Unix files..." William Brandel, *Digital Review*.

11/23/87   "**Oracle Corp.** last week announced that the **Oracle 5.1** database manager for **OS/2** will ship in January...'Now that **IBM** has committed to shipping their new operating system in early December, Oracle will be able to almost immediately deliver the first multitasking SQL DBMS for that environment.'" Scott Mace, *Info World*.

11/17/87   "The database component of **IBM's OS/2 Extended Edition**...contains a Query Manager for updating and querying a database using Structured Query Language (SQL), a report generator and a utility for exchanging data with personal computer applications." Beth Freedman, *PC Week*.

11/17/87   "**Microrim Inc.**, maker of the **R:base** relational database, is preparing a family of new DOS and OS/2 products that supports Structured Query Language (SQL)...Microrim's vice president of marketing, Marco Hegyi, said the company is committed to bringing out SQL products to satisfy its users' demands...The addition of embedded SQL commands in future Microrim products is essential for corporations with distributed, PC-based information systems..." Jim Forbes and Beth Freedman, *PC Week*.

11/16/87   "**Tandem Computer Inc.**'s fault-tolerant minicomputers are likely to offer mainframe performance when running the company's new relational database management system (RDBMS)...Tandem's **NonStop SQL DBMS**...endows the NonStop computers with high-speed transaction processing and programming tools..." Irwin Greenstein, *MIS Week*.

11/16/87   "Many functions of **IBM's DB2** and **SQL/DS** mainframe database products are included in IBM's **OS/2 Extended**

Edition Database Manager. The Database Manager supports the relational data model, storing information in a series of tables..." Alice LaPlante, *Info World*.

11/16/87   "**Novell Inc.** and data base management developer **Oracle Corp.** have revealed a plan to integrate their products and form networked distributed data management systems for personal computers... Oracle will run its Structured Query Language-based data base management system on Novell's **NetWare** operating system across different local area networks." Charlie Bruno and Joshua Greenbaum, *Communications Week*.

11/15/87   "No discussion in the relational realm would be complete without a look at SQL, the relational data access from **IBM**. The standardization of this language will provide enormous benefits in communications between systems and in adaptability of both software and people skills. In theory at least, SQL will give users an open architecture for database management for the first time... Both ANSI and the International Standards Organization have adopted SQL as the standard language for relational database systems access. The Department of Defense has also thrown its weight behind SQL, mandating the language's inclusion in future procurements." George Schussel, *Datamation*.

11/10/87   "**Visual Software** has enriched its computer-aided software-engineering (CASE) tools... through the use of **vsSQL Advanced Query/Report Generator**, software designers can use the Structured Query Language (SQL) to query and analyze their database designs... 'We decided this whole issue of how you analyze the contents of the database is one that needs to be tackled from a query language... SQL is much more robust than anything else that exists in the market, in terms of its analysis capabilities. And, since it is SQL, and other products on the mainframe use SQL, that gives us a bridge to other software.'" Kathleen Doler, *PC Week*.

11/10/87   "Downloading information from a mainframe or minicomputer database into popular PC applications is now possible with new Structured Query Language (SQL) software from **DB/Access**. The program, called **View/PC**, is written with **Microsoft Corp.**'s graphical Windows environment and can be used to take data from a host running DB/Access's **Access/**

Star SQL database and create PC files in four common data formats..." *PC Week.*

11/9/87   "**DEC** gave its relational database users an enhanced query language late last month, as well as an expanded reach into **IBM** mainframes... announced was version 1.1 of **VAX SQL**, DEC's implementation of the ANSI-standard structured query language. VAX SQL is designed as an interface to **Rdb/VMS** databases... 'The important message here is that we're moving right along on our strategy of full support of the ANSI standard and maximal use of the Digital architecture,' a DEC spokesman said." Nell Margolis, *Digital Review.*

11/9/87   "**Informix Software** launched a bevy of software announcements recently... 'We see OS/2 as a key component of **IBM**'s Systems Application Architecture (SAA) and we intend to provide SQL-based data base front ends across all six operating systems [OS/2, Unix, MS-DOS, VMS, MVS and VM] and SAA SQL-compatible data base engines where IBM does not provide them,' said Roger Sippl, Informix president." George Abruzzese, *Computer & Software News.*

11/9/87   "Among the highlights at last month's **Unix Expo** trade show... A new release of **Focus 4GL/DBMS** from **Information Builders Inc.** of New York, includes an SQL translator and improves the portability of applications and data files across different hardware platforms." William Brandel, *Digital Review.*

11/87   **SQL Software**, located in Cleveland, Ohio, has announced "release 1.40 of **Structured Query Report Writer (SQR)**... currently available for the **Oracle** database on VAX/VMS, IBM PC, and DG-MV/AOS; a key component is the ability to combine SQL query definition with print control, formatting, and procedural logic..." *Hardcopy.*

11/9/87   "**Software AG** of North America, a major software developer in the **IBM** market, is looking to expand its role in the **DEC** market dramatically... Although Software AG's two core products—**Adabas** and **Natural**—have been available to DEC users for three years, this week's announcement's signaled a turning point... **Adabas SQL**, another new tool, is used for defining and processing data in Adabas. Within an application program, SQL command clauses generate in-line communications with Adabas using a simple, easy-to-master syntax."

Kristiina Sorensen, *Digital Review.*

11/9/87   "Software gateways to **RMS** and **dBase** data files will be the maiden entries in **Relational Technology Inc.**'s new product line, aimed at linking yesterday's file management systems to today's relational database management technology in order to create tomorrow's fully distributed database environments ... **Ingres dBase Gateway** ... will provide SQL access to dBase files stored in **PC-DOS** and **MS-DOS** microcomputer environments ... Further gateways are foreseen to such file management systems as **IMS, Rdb,** and **DB2.**" Nell Margolis, *Digital Review.*

11/3/87   "Because SQL is regarded by industry experts as the most efficient way to retrieve data from PC, minicomputer and mainframe, many software companies have embraced it as a common data-access language and are incorporating SQL support into their products ... 'SQL is ... a revolution for the people who think that the database systems of the future will be connected ones.'" Beth Freedman, *PC Week.*

11/3/87   "**Oracle Corp.** has brought its first computer-aided software engineering (CASE) tools to market, offering customers software power to help them automate and manage building and maintenance of the Oracle Structured Query Language (SQL) compatible relational database systems." *PC Week.*

11/2/87   "Users of the nonrelational databases, **RMS** and **dBase III**, can unite their existing data with a relational database management system and access the older data files through structured query language commands with software that **Relational Technology Inc.** is announcing today. RTI of Alameda, Calif., is introducing **RMS Gateway** amd **dBase Gateway**, software that the company says provides a migration path from 'early generation file management systems,' such as **Digital Equipment Corp.**'s RMS for VAXs and **Ashton-Tate Co.**'s dBase III for personal computers ... the new products permit users to access RMS and dBase III files using SQL ..." Don Kennedy, *Digital News.*

11/1/87   "The early word is positive on **Tandem Computers Inc.**'s new **NonStop SQL** distributed relational database ... A few early bugs in the new RDBMS have been fixed and the system is meeting expectations." *Datamation.*

10/87   "In an effort to redefine the performance standards of relational database management, **Britton Lee Inc.** (Los Gatos, Calif.) made several potent product announcements...Most newsworthy was the **BL8000 Shared Database System**, a 32-bit machine based on both parallel processing and reduced instruction set computer (RISC) concepts...V. 2 of the company's Integrated Database Manager (IDM) was also introduced to accomodate the BL8000's 32-bit architecture. Conforming to ANSI SQL and DB2 (both industry standards), V. 2 consists of the IDM host-resident sotfware and IDM/RDBMS that resides in the Britton Lee hardware." Evan Birkhead, *Hardcopy.*

10/26/87   "**Informix Software** has introduced **Informix-ESQL/Ada**, a software development tool designed to meet the growing demand of application developers who must comply with government standards for the Ada programming language. Informix-ESQL/Ada...was created to meet the need for database management and application development software based on ANSI-standard SQL for Ada..." Laura DiDio, *Digital Review.*

10/26/87   "Lawrence J. Ellison, the president and biggest shareholder of **Oracle Corp.**, isn't being modest when he predicts his pioneering database management company will be 'the fastest-growing software company in the world.'...The seven-year-old structured query language (SQL) developer has enjoyed explosive growth since its start, catching the need for professionals to access multiple databases from a minicomputer...One key strategy will be to maintain **Oracle**'s absolute compatibility with **IBM Corp.**'s SQL offering but to ensure that it remains portable down to the mini- and microcomputer level, unlike **IBM SQL**." David Zielenziger, *Electronic Engineering Times.*

10/26/87   "...**InterBase Software Corp.** rolled out the second version of its 1-year-old **InterBase** relational database management system...included in this latest edition is support for dynamic SQL (DSQL), which lets programs build queries at run time..." Nell Margolis, *Digital Review.*

10/26/87   "...**Informix Corp.** and **Innovative Software Inc.** announced recently their intent to merge...The combination of Innovative's **Smart Software System**, a line of micro and minicomputer business applications, and Informix's database technology should open the door to a series of modular office automation products—word processing, graphics, communications, and electronic mail—all having companywide access to local or centralized databases via an SQL interface, company officials said." Carole Patton, *Info World*.

10/87   "Two of the industry's leading database management system (DBMS) packages are now available from **Elxsi** (San Jose, Calif.). Recently signed marketing agreements with **Oracle Corp.** and **Relational Technology Inc.**—made in an effort to reach the large database-user market—provide availability of **ORACLE** and **Ingres DBMS** software on the **System 6400**." Renee P. Brown, *Hardcopy*.

10/20/87   "'SQL is the relational DBMS standard,' according to Steve Vandor, PC marketing product manager at **Relational Technology Inc.**, of Alameda, Calif., makers of the **Ingres** database...'If there is one language that is common among different kinds of machines, SQL is it. You just send the same SQL request up to the host and ship the results down to the user transparently.'" Vincent Puglia, *PC Week*.

10/19/87   "**Blyth Software** recently announced it would support **Sybase Inc.**'s **SQL Dataserver** technology in future Macintosh product development, reinforcing growing ties between the Mac world and Structured Query Language (SQL)." Scott Mace, *Info World*.

10/87   "Software vendor **Applied Data Research** (ADR) unveiled five new major products and product enhancements in September. These included versions of its data base management software (DBMS) that support **IBM's DB2** and **SQL DBMS** standards...the new versions reflect the emerging acceptance of SQL and DB2 as industry standards." *Infosystems*.

10/19/87   "Even before they know details about the database component of **IBM's OS/2** Extended Edition, database publishers plan a...response...**Sybase**, a Berkeley, California, developer of a server-requester database system for Unix systems, is working on an OS/2 product that, like IBM's Extended Edition, provides an SQL interface and database management...**IBM's** prime goal is to provide a standard SQL interface so workstations running OS/2 can communicate with IBM minicomputers and mainframes..." Scott Mace, *Info World*.

10/19/87   "**Informix Corp.** and **Innovative Software Inc.** last week said they had executed a letter of intent to merge   Michael

J. Brown [cofounder of Innovative]... said, 'We believe that successful future Office Automation offerings will include the ability to interconnect to larger departmental and company-wide computer systems and their respective databases through an SQL interface.'" Theresa Conlon, *MIS Week*.

10/13/87 "**Network Innovations Corp.** recently introduced a program to extract data from **Oracle Corp.**'s SQL databases and format it for use in popular PC application programs, including **Lotus Development Corp.**'s **1-2-3** and **Ashton-Tate**'s **dBASE**. Called **Multiplex/PC**, the program... allows users to browse through and extract data from the mainframe- or minicomputer-based databases interactively." *PC Week*.

10/13/87 "A new product from **Gupta Technologies Inc.** merges the efficient data-retrieval capabilities of the Structured Query Language (SQL) with the ease of use and graphics features of **Microsoft Windows**. Called **SQLWindows**, the package is a fourth-generation development tool that allows programmers to develop sophisticated database applications that incorporate SQL retrieval techniques..." Beth Freedman, *PC Week*.

10/12/87 "Although new product introductions have never been a hallmark of the annual **Federal Computer Conference** (FCC), it continues to attract the computer industry's most extensive assortment of government bureaucrats, top-brass and third-party contractors. Dominating the immediate attention of attendees... was the competition among several database software suppliers for one of the largest government contracts of the year. The winner of the database contest, darkhorse vendor **Applied Data Research** (ADR) of Princeton, N.J., was awarded a U.S. Army contract to supply 75,000 copies of an SQL relational database management system (RDBMS) for **Unix** systems." Michael Vizard, *Digital Review*.

10/12/87 "**DB/Access** has introduced **View/PC**, a new module of its **Access/Star** connectivity products that adds personal computer access to information stored in minicomputer and mainframe databases... The Access/Star data sharing software uses standard SQL as a data access language..." *MIS Week*.

10/12/87 "**Signal Technology Inc.** has introduced version 5.1 of its **Smartstar** fourth-generation language (4GL) application development system, which is designed specifically to run desktop data management on the VAX/VMS operating system...Smartstar is Signal's SQL-based applications development system designed exclusively for VAX/VMS and in-depth compatibility with the VAX information architecture. It includes both interactive and programmable SQL..." Laura DiDio, *Digital Review*.

10/12/87   "Computer Associates International announced that the latest version of its relational database management system, **CA-Universe**, supports the SQL standard...CA-Universe is available for all **IBM** mainframes running DOS, MVS, or VM." *Information Week*.

10/12/87   "In the first effort to link **VAX**es with supercomputer-class database management hardware, **Teradata Corp.** has introduced a connectivity package that lets VAX/VMS systems directly access the resources of Teradata's high-performance **DBC/1012 Data Base Computer**. Called the **VAX Interface**, the new software package works in conjunction with an Ethernet local area network...to provide a transparent gateway between VAX computers and the DBC/1012 SQL relational database management system." Terry C. Shannon, *Digital Review*.

10/12/87   "As **Microsoft** announced the PC version of **Excel**, other software vendors quickly offered database extensions, several using the spreadsheet's Dynamic Data Exchange facility. **Multiplex/XL** from **Network Innovations Corp.** lets Excel users select an added 'host' menu option and, through Windows dialog boxes, enter SQL statements directly into the spreadsheet from data on VAX or UNIX systems." Edward Warner, *Info World*.

10/12/87   "Fireworks in the sky marked the end of **Cullinet Software Inc.**'s annual User Week...Among the brightest product shots fired off: Cullinet's entry into the **VAX**-based relational DBMS market, **IDMS/SQL**, which...is slated for commercial availability in the first quarter of 1988." Nell Margolis, *Digital Review*.

10/6/87   "**Oracle Corp.** is rewriting its PC structured-query-language (SQL) database for OS/2, providing faster processing speeds and a graphical user interface...Company officials also gave users a preview of a new add-in for Lotus 1-2-3 called **1-2-SQL**. Scheduled for debut in December, 1-2-SQL will let Lotus

1-2-3 make SQL queries on an Oracle PC database from 1-2-3 worksheets ... " Beth Freedman, *PC Week*.

10/5/87   "**Pansophic Systems Inc.** has released a new interface to **IBM**'s **DB2** and **SQL/DS** database management systems that gives Pansophic's **Gener/OL** users a **CICS** application development ... Pansophic said the new **Gener/OL DB2 SQL/DS** interface provided access to data through a full complement of 'static' SQL commands consistent with IBM standards." *MIS Week*.

10/5/87   "A multiuser, SQL-based database management system has been announced for the Macintosh II running the Unixlike A/UX operating system ... two other **Informix** products will be ported to the Macintosh II, including ... a new program, called **Informix-Esql/Ada**, which embeds SQL commands into the Ada programming language—a language that is used heavily in the federal marketplace." Scott Mace, *Info World*.

10/5/87   "This year marks a turning point for relational data base management systems. The reason: a standard interface is about to make relational data base management systems interchangeable. Known as the Structured Query Language (SQL), the interface has been blessed not only by IBM and the American National Standards Institute but also by the U.S. government and international standards organizations." Nancy Lundell, *Information Week*.

10/5/87   "3:20 p.m., Thurs., **Applied Data Research Inc.**, Princeton, N.J., signs an agreement to supply up to 75,000 **XDS** SQL-based relational database-management microcomputer software packages developed by **Software Systems Technologies Inc.**, College Park, Md., to all U.S. Army Standard Management Information Systems sites." *MIS Week*.

10/5/87   " ... These two forces—open architectures and standards—are the deep, fundamental reasons for the sudden prominence of SQL ... By separating front-end tools and applications from the SQL data base engines, SQL eases user concerns about proprietary, closed architectures and vendor lock-ins ... Another aspect of SQL is that it enables developers to create cooperative processing applications where the user interface resides on one system (say a PC) while the data resides on another (say a mainframe.) Applications or systems on the two machines link the two 'SQL engines.'" Michael Braude, *Information Week*.

10/5/87   "**Cullinet Software Inc.**, one of the largest vendors in the **IBM Corp.** mainframe market, is poised to formally enter the mainstream VAX market with a newly developed relational database that uses structured query language...The new product, **IDMS/SQL**, will be introduced along with a fourth-generation tool kit and code generator...[Marketing vice president] Papows said IBM users are looking for an alternative to IBM's **DB/2** database, but do not want to change their existing hardware, which often includes VAXs. With IDMS/SQL and its related products, he said, IBM users now can port files directly from the mainframe to the departmental system without file conversion problems..." Stephan Lawton, *Digital News*.

10/5/87   "**Oracle** has entered the **computer-aided software engineering** market with two products: the SQL*Development Method, which is designed to help create a systematic environment of business applications; and the SQL*Design Dictionary, which provides tools for users who want to design or better document and control applications. The products are available for VAX/VMS environments: MS-DOS and MVS/XA versions are nearing completion." *Information Week*.

10/5/87   "Now that its **R-DBMS** for the VAX and its multipart banking system are established, **Cullinet Software Inc.** of Westwood, Mass., is once again behaving like an entrepreneurial company...**IDMS/R** Release 10.2, which contains full SQL support for on-line query, will be available later this year. With Release 11, to be beta tested in late '88, Cullinet will consider IDMS/R fully relational." Diana ben-Aaron, *Information Week*.

10/1/87   "After a shaky start four years ago, **DB2**—IBM's relational database management system—has become a legend in its own time...Independent database vendors are busily scrambling around, trying to prove how their products either enhance or surpass DB2...One aspect of DB2 that's getting critical acclaim is SQL. Digital Consulting's Schussel calls SQL the 'most salient feature of DB2.' Both ANSI and ISO have adopted SQL as a standard. Thus, Schussel predicts that those independents who have been slower to support SQL 'will be hurting over the next two or three years, or until they are able to support SQL.'" Edith D. Myers, *Datamation*.

10/1/87   "Relational DBMS vendor **Oracle Corp.** will soon jump into the fray that is developing among suppliers of transaction-oriented database management systems... The new product will be positioned to compete with **Tandem Computer Inc.**'s **Non-Stop SQL** high-performance transaction DBMS and a database system from Berkeley startup **Sybase Inc.**" *Datamation*.

9/29/87   "The next release of **Ashton-Tate**'s **dBASE** will incorporate Structured Query Language (SQL) commands, allowing users to manipulate data in dBASE applications with the industry-standard query language... SQL is seen throughout the industry as an efficient means of manipulating data within an application and as a mechanism for communicating data among mainframes, minis and PCs." Beth Freedman, *PC Week*.

9/28/87   "In 1970, Dr. E.F. Codd, currently president of the The Relational Institute, published a now-classic paper that proposed the **relational model** for database management... Codd supports the development of industry standards but considers the caliber of the current offering far from adequate. He considers **IBM**'s SQL only 50% relational... 'I am in favor of extending IBM's SQL, but it is important to keep IBM's as a base to facilitate compatibility.' Although IBM's SQL is widely recognized as being far from perfect, it is generally acknowledged as being here to stay. 'To say you're not going to have an SQL front end is saying you're not going to compete in the database world,' says John Logan, a senior analyst with the Yankee Group." Christopher Maynard, *Information Week*.

9/28/87   "**Borland** is making big plans to showcase its **Ansa** subsidiary's **Paradox** product... Ansa will deliver a Paradox product letting pc users transparently access data stored on SQL-based mini and mainframe computer systems... Doug Cayne, analyst for The Gartner Group, Stamford, Conn., said the SQL development was the 'real key to future success' in reaching the corporate marketplace." *Computer & Software News*.

9/21/87   "**Applied Data Research Inc.** (ADR), an **IBM** mainframe-based systems software company, last week became the first major production-oriented database management system (DBMS) vendor to announce SQL support in its flagship DBMS product—**Datacom/DB**—making it what analysts called 'the first real plug-compatible alternative' to IBM's relational DBMS, **DB/2** ... 'The strategic direction users should stay in touch with isn't DB2, it's SQL...SQL is the key to independence from any one DBMS.'" Theresa Conlon, *MIS Week*.

9/21/87   "**Oracle Corp.** has signed an agreement with the **Hewlett-Packard Co.** to provide its relational DBMS (RDBMS) software for the HP 3000 series 900 business computers. The agreement makes **Oracle** the first third-party RDBMS to be announced for both the new HP 3000 series 900 business systems and the HP 9000 scientific systems ... " *MIS Week*.

9/21/87   "In an announcement designed to reinforce its commitment to the high-end corporate market, **Borland** last week said its **Ansa** subsidiary is developing five versions of **Paradox**... Versions of Paradox for OS/2, Presentation Manager, Windows 2.0, and Unix, as well as support for SQL, will be available during the first half of 1988, officials said." Rachael Parker, *Info World*.

9/21/87   "**Software AG** of North America has expanded the capabilities of its **Natural 2** fourth-generation (4GL) application development system to include support for **IBM's DB2** and **SQL/DS** databases... A company spokesman said, 'The delivery of Natural 2 functionality to the DB2, SQL/DS operating environments is yet another step in Software AG's plan to provide full SQL support throughout its database and application development system product solutions.'" *MIS Week*.

9/14/87   "By selecting **Informix Software Inc.** to provide the strategic relational database management system (RDBMS) for its complete line of **Unix System V**-based computers, **AT&T** has gained 'the equivalent of **IBM's** Systems Application Architecture (SAA) and SQL for **AT&T** computers'... **Informix** brings to **AT&T** an SQL database engine that runs well on all different-size **AT&T** machines ... " Theresa Conlon, *MIS Week*.

9/14/87   "**Oracle Corp.** has announced "the prospective release later this year of SQL-QMX, a clone of **IBM's** QMF query and reporting facility. SQL-QMX runs on **IBM** mainframes, as well as on PCs and **DEC** VAX minicomputers. It can thus be marketed to **IBM** mainframe shops as a tool with which new users are already familiar... A new product, SQL-Connect, will permit **Oracle** tools such as SQL-Plus and SQL-QMX and applications written with these tools to access **DB2**, rather than **Oracle** as a database." Mike Feuche, *MIS Week*.

9/7/87   "**Honeywell Bull** will distribute a Structured Query Language (SQL) enhancement to its **ONEbase** database management system (DBMS) as the result of an agreement with **DB/ Access Inc.**... **Access/Star** will enable **ONEbase** users to extract data from remote databases such as **IBM DB2**, and **Digital Equipment Corp.**'s **Rdb** and **DBMS**, for example, and load data into **Oracle Corp.**'s relational DBMS..." *MIS Week*.

9/87   "**Rhodnius' Empress** relational database software is rooted in pioneer design work done at the University of Toronto during the late 1970s... To broaden the product's appeal further, Rhodnius ported **Empress** from UNIX to VAX/VMS and PC/ MS-DOS in 1986... and now hopes to sell **Empress** as a general relational database against competitors like **Oracle** and **Ingres**... The product's QUERY facility is an extended ANSI-standard SQL, with full data definition and manipulation syntax." Al Cini, *DEC Professional*.

9/87   "**Oracle Corp.**, Belmont, Calif., makers of **Oracle**, a leading relational database management system (RDBMS), formed a financial service industry marketing group... Since **Oracle** is an SQL-based program it will be compatible with **IBM**'s new OS/2 extended operating system... **Microsoft** is designing a proprietary operating system for **IBM** which incorporates an SQL-based relational database management system... any Wall Street firm wishing to develop an application that feeds off an RDBMS need not wait for IBM's 1988 release of OS/2. They can choose Oracle, which supports the SQL approved by the American National Standards Institute (ANSI), also adopted by IBM for its **DB/2** mainframe program." *Wall Street Computer Review*.

8/31/87   "**Apple Computer Inc.** last week said it will make a minority investment through its Strategic Investment Group in **Sybase Inc.**, a Berkeley, Calif., developer of a relational database management system... Apple's investment will in turn yield Sybase for the Macintosh... When available, it will bring Structured Query Language (SQL) capabilities to the Macintosh family." Irwin Greenstein, *MIS Week*.

8/31/87   "**Apple Computer Inc.** is investing in **Sybase Inc.**, a new DBMS vendor ... The new partnership should not change Sybase's overall direction, but it is an important move for Apple as it positions itself to sell the new Macintosh II and Macintosh SE against **IBM**'s **PS/2**, which will eventually be equipped with an SQL-based DBMS conforming to IBM's Systems Applications Architecture." Diana ben-Aaron, *Information Week*.

8/24/87   "New York—**Britton Lee Inc.** used last month's National Financial Computer and Automation Conference here to debut its BL8000 Shared Database System, a new 32-bit high-end database machine ... also announced were ... the unbundling of Britton Lee's **Integrated Database Manager (IDM)** software, the system software that runs on the vendor's database machines ... Britton Lee is developing an enhanced version of the **IDM** software that will support **IBM**'s **DB2** DBMS as well as the ANSI Structured Query Language (SQL) standard. The new system software, which will allow VAXes and IBM personal computers to access and share SQL-compliant databases, is expected to be available within a year." Terry C. Shannon, *Digital Review*.

8/24/87   "A data entry control language is one of the features of **Condor 4**, the working name for **Condor Computer Corp.**'s successor to the **Condor 3** database manager ... Condor 4 allows users to create larger databases ... and adds more text handling functions and user variables. Expanded SQL-like Where clauses have also been added, the company said." Scott Mace, *Info World*.

8/17/87   "**Borland** officials discussed future plans and the effect of the **Ansa** merger ... A key feature will be **Turbo** languages' capability to access data files from **Paradox**, the firm's high-end database product ... Paradox, the product Borland picked up with the recent Ansa merger, will not only be accessible from Borland's languages but will likely have an SQL option. An SQL interface to relational data is to be included in **IBM**'s **OS/2 Extended Edition** and is considered by some to be a critical feature for competition in that segment of the market." Jeff Angus, *InfoWorld*.

8/10/87   "Combining elements of **Pick**, **Oracle**, and **DB2**, **Unidata Inc.** will shortly release a multiuser database management system running under **Xenix** and **Unix**...The new database system—also called **Unidata**—will feature Pick file structure compatibility, ANSI-standard SQL, and an English data manipulation language." David Brunel, president of **Unidata**, states that "This is more than just Pick under Unix though...We are offering the large Pick library of business applications and their user-friendliness but adding to that the power of ANSI-standard SQL ..." Mark Stephens, *Info World*.

8/3/87   "The success of a distributed DBMS system hinges largely on the efficiency of its networking...Standardization throughout the system is important. You need good, standard communications protocols...And you need a standard query language, such as the widely implemented SQL (structured query language), so all the databases in the distributed architecture can talk to one another." Bill Brindley, *Digital Review*.

8/3/87   "**Britton Lee Inc.** has extended its line of database systems with new models that the company says will allow **VAX**s and **IBM** Personal Computers to share relational databases that use structured query language (SQL)." Mary Boston, *Digital News*.

7/28/87   "To paraphrase C.J. Date, one of the chief proponents of relational database management systems: Vendors seem to have fallen in love with Structured Query Language (SQL)...Following **IBM**'s Extended Edition announcements and the recent standardization of the SQL language from the American National Standards Institute (ANSI), users are faced with two questions: 'Do I need SQL?' and 'Which SQL-based standard should I follow?'" Vincent Puglia, *PC Week*.

7/28/87   "Despite—or perhaps because of—its multicomponent nature, its powerful implementation of the Structured Query Language (SQL) and its easy-to-use query and report generators, **Ingres** for the PC may require some reassessment on the part of PC users who want to use it as a stand-alone RDBMS, but it is an elegant solution for those users who want all the power they can handle...It provides power and control over data that traditional PC DBMSs cannot offer." Vincent Puglia, *PC Week*.

7/27/87   "Harry K. T. Wong, **Ashton-Tate Corp.**'s newly appointed senior scientist, has emerged as a key figure in the drive to port Structured Query Language (SQL) to the company's **dBase** family, the de facto standard in DOS databases ... 'Deep down, we believe that SQL and **dBase** should be married together,' Wong said. 'All of our tests and experiments indicate that a much more powerful environment is created through this union...'" Irwin Greenstein, *MIS Week.*

7/20/87   "**Cullinet Software Inc.** is headed straight for the VAX market, fulfilling a promise it made last year. The company says its first product for the VAX, a relational database management system called **IDMS/SQL**, will be released this fall... George Colony, president of Forrester Research Inc., a market research firm in Cambridge, Mass., says **Cullinet** is 'betting the company on' **IDMS/SQL**." Kathryn Esplin, *Digital News.*

7/14/87   One advantage of **IBM**'s new microcomputer operating system, **OS/2**, is "its ability to run database-management programs that conform to SQL, the standard database-application development language... while SQL database systems were formerly confined to mainframes, 'You can see everybody scrambling' to produce SQL-compatible programs for the PC." Amy Gorin, *PC Week.*

7/14/87   A new version of the popular microcomputer database product, **dBASE**, "will feature a database engine that provides the performance of minicomputer database programs, and extended **dBASE** language with SQL and transparent connectivity to departmental and corporate computers." Beth Freedman, *PC Week.*

7/14/87   "With new versions of **dBASE** well on their way, **Ashton-Tate** is dressing up **Framework** with similar functionality. Support for local area networks and the Structured Query Language (SQL) are two of the key new features slated for the next release of the five-module integrated program..." *PC Week.*

7/13/87   "**Oracle Corp.** of Belmont, California, maker of the **Oracle** relational database, said it will mimic the entire functionality of OS/2 Extended Edition. **Oracle** will move existing **IBM**-compatible SQL and SNA PC-to-mainframe networking programs to OS/2..." Scott Mace, *InfoWorld.*

7/13/87   "**IBM**'s relational database **DB2** now scores a little more than its main rivals on most key criteria, according to a confidential report by one of Britain's largest all-Blue shops, IMI computing... the firm evaluated **Cullinet**'s **IBMS/X**, **Software AG**'s **Adabas**, **ADR**'s **Datacom**, **CCA**'s **Model 204**,

Oracle and Ingres...DB2 compared favorably with most of them in being highly relational, fairly easy to adapt to existing applications, and in particular on its security and recovery features." Philip Hunter, *Information Week*.

7/7/87   **Lotus Development Corp.** will announce that a new version of its micro-to-mainframe link product, **The Application Connection, (T-A-C)**, will allow microcomputer users to query **IBM**'s relational databse **DB2** using the spreadsheat program **1-2-3**. *PC Week*.

7/6/87   "**Gupta Technologies, Inc.** is expected to release this month a distributed networking product that can tie together different vendors' SQL-based data base management systems on different-sized machines." The product, **SQL Net**, working in conjunction with a related product, **SQL Base,** will allow microcomputer users to query mainframe relational databases. Charles Babcock, *Computerworld*.

7/6/87   Release 3, the latest version of **IBM**'s relational database product **DB2** adds some needed features but fails to provide others. Date and time fields are supported. Not supported are: referential integrity; an integrated and active data dictionary; updates of tables through update of views. Shaku Atre, *Computerworld*.

7/87   "You can't escape SQL," headlines an article in *Information Center* by Nick Rawlings, which recommends that people working in an **IBM** computer environment prepare themselves for an "SQL landslide" and "jump on the SQL freight train."

7/87   "Wall Street goes relational: demand for high performance relational database management systems is an emerging niche on Wall Street...In the past users were willing to sacrifice speed for flexibility in a database system. But, now brokerage houses demand both qualities..." **The Security Pacific Corp.** has developed a "state-of-the-art trading application" using a DEC VAX minicomputer, the C language, and SQL. Ivy Schmerken, *Wall Street Computer Review*.

7/87   **The Arity Corp.,** makers of an interpreter and compiler for the artificial intelligence language PROLOG, are now providing **Arity/SQL,** a product which will allow the embedding of SQL statements within PROLOG programs. Marc Rettig, *AI Expert*.

6/29/87 Kudos for **Ingres**, a leading SQL-database: "Clearly the performance results for Ingres are quite remarkable. Thirty-five users all simultaneously accessing a local database and performing updates, CPU-intensive set functions and three-table joins without excessive time delays is an impressive achievement." *Digital Review.*

6/29/87 A leading SQL-database vendor, **The Oracle Corp.**, announced a marketing and product development relationship with **Sequent Computer Systems, inc.**, a manufacturer of parallel-processor computers. "A product that weds Oracle distributed database features to the high-throughput capacity mandated by heavily multiuser transaction processing applications has been under development for approximately two years..." Neil Margolis, *Digital Review.*

6/15/87 "**Softcraft Inc.** has announced an SQL database manager designed to enhance the performance of its **Btrieve** file management system used by programmers for creating databases." Scott Mace, *Infoworld.*

6/9/87 "We plan to embed SQL capabilities within the familiar Dbase user interface and develop transparent links between the two that will allow the user to access SQL's strengths without having to struggle with its deficiencies," says Edward Esber, chairman and chief executive officer of **Ashton-Tate**, makers of the popular **Dbase** microcomputer database software. *Infoworld.*

6/8/87 Preliminary testing has proved successful for an SQL-based relational database management system introduced last year by **Sybase Inc.** "It's the first time that someone has been able to show that a relational DBMS can handle an on-line transaction system...It's able to provide the relational query capabilities that all the others provide, but it also has very fast update facilities." Rosemary Hamilton, *Computerworld.*

6/1/87 "**IBM** was blasted by Chris Date, one of the two founding fathers of relational database technology, for confusing users by continuing to enhance its older IMS database while failing to deliver the expected upgrades to **DB2**...Date echoed the disappointment of many users by pointing to IBM's failure to introduce referential integrity into DB2..." *InformationWeek.*

Appendix E: Bibliography

1. American National Standards Institute. *Database Language–SQL.* American National Standards Institute, Inc., Document ANSI X3.135-1986. New York, 1986.

    This is *the* standard, and describes the features which should be provided in any SQL implementation. Many features which have already been offered by various vendors were not included in the standard. There is already talk of an extended standard. The standard is intended for designers who wish to implement SQL, is highly technical, and does not make for casual reading.

2. Oracle Corporation. *SQL*Plus User's Guide.* Oracle Corporation, Document 3201-V1.0. Belmont, California, 1986.

    The user's manual for a commercial SQL implementation, one which offers many features not included in the standard.

3. C.J. Date. *Relational Database: Selected Writings.* Addison-Wesley Publishing Co., Inc. 1986.

4. C.J. Date. *A Guide to the SQL Standard.* Addison-Wesley Publishing Co., Inc. 1987.

5. C.J. Date. *A Guide to DB2.* Addison-Wesley Publishing Co., Inc. 1984.

    A discussion of a commercial SQL implementation, IBM's relational database DB2.

6. C.J. Date. *Database: A Primer.* Addison-Wesley Publishing Co., Inc. 1983.

    In general, C.J. Date's work is addressed to designers and programmers, but the serious reader will find all of the books accessible and rewarding. The volumes above are only a partial listing of his work.

Appendix F: SQL Quick Reference

— SIMPLE QUERIES —

SELECT * FROM TBLA;

SELECT DISTINCT FLDA FROM TBLA;

SELECT FLDA, FLDB FROM TBLA;

SELECT * FROM TBLA WHERE FLDA = 10;

SELECT FLDA FROM TBLA WHERE FLDA > 10;

SELECT FLDA, FLDB FROM TBLA WHERE FLDA < 10;

SELECT FLDA FROM TBLA WHERE FLDA <> 10;

SELECT * FROM TBLA WHERE FLDA <= 10;

SELECT FLDA FROM TBLA WHERE FLDA >= 10;

SELECT FLDA FROM TBLA WHERE FLDA IS NULL;

SELECT FLDA FROM TBLA WHERE FLDA IS NOT NULL;

SELECT * FROM TBLA WHERE
FLDC IN (10, 25, 30, 105);

SELECT * FROM TBLA WHERE
(FLDC = 10 AND FLDD < 150);

SELECT * FROM TBLA WHERE
(FLDD < 25 OR FLDD > 100);

— SIMPLE QUERIES —

SELECT * FROM TBLA WHERE FLDA = 'Blue';

SELECT FLDA FROM TBLA WHERE FLDA > 'Y';

SELECT DISTINCT FLDA FROM TBLA WHERE FLDA > 'Y';

SELECT FLDA, FLDB FROM TBLA WHERE FLDA < 'Gr';

SELECT FLDA FROM TBLA WHERE FLDA
IN ('Orange', 'Yellow', 'Brown');

SELECT FLDA FROM TBLA WHERE FLDA LIKE '%';

SELECT FLDA FROM TBLA WHERE FLDA LIKE 'B%';

SELECT FLDA FROM TBLA WHERE FLDA LIKE 'B___';

SELECT FLDA FROM TBLA WHERE FLDA LIKE 'B_u_';

SELECT FLDA FROM TBLA WHERE FLDA LIKE 'B_u%';

SELECT FLDA FROM TBLA WHERE FLDA LIKE 'Or_n_%';

SELECT FLDA FROM TBLA WHERE FLDA IS NULL;

SELECT FLDA FROM TBLA WHERE FLDA IS NOT NULL;

— USING OPERATORS —

SELECT (FLDA + FLDB) FROM TBLA;

SELECT (FLDA / 2.5) FROM TBLA;

SELECT ((FLDA − FLDB) * 5) FROM TBLA;

SELECT MAX(FLDA) FROM TBLA;

SELECT MIN(FLDA + FLDB) FROM TBLA;

SELECT COUNT(*) FROM TBLA;

SELECT COUNT(FLDA) FROM TBLA;

SELECT COUNT(FLDA) FROM TBLA
WHERE FLDA > 34;

SELECT SUM(FLDA) FROM TBLA;

SELECT AVG(FLDA) FROM TBLA;

— QUERYING MULTIPLE TABLES —

SELECT FLDA, FLDB FROM TBLA, TBLB;

SELECT FLDA, FLDB FROM TBLA, TBLB
WHERE FLDA = FLDB;

SELECT TBLA.FLDA, TBLB.FLDA FROM TBLA, TBLB;

SELECT TBLA.FLDA, TBLB.FLDA FROM TBLA, TBLB
WHERE TBLA.FLDA >= TBLB.FLDA

SELECT FLDA, FLDB FROM TBLA, TBLB
WHERE (FLDA = FLDB) OR
(FLDA IS NULL AND FLDB IS NULL);

SELECT FLDA, FLDB FROM TBLA, TBLB
WHERE (FLDA > FLDB) AND (FLDB < 35);

— SUBQUERIES —

SELECT FLDA FROM TBLA
WHERE FLDA = (SELECT FLDB FROM TBLB);

SELECT FLDA FROM TBLA
WHERE FLDA IN (SELECT FLDB FROM TBLB);

SELECT FLDA FROM TBLA
WHERE FLDA =
(SELECT FLDB FROM TBLB WHERE FLDC = 'Green');

SELECT FLDA, FLDB FROM TBLA
WHERE FLDA > 25 AND
FLDB IN (SELECT FLDC FROM TBLC);

SELECT FLDA FROM TBLA
WHERE FLDA > ANY (SELECT FLDB FROM TBLB);

SELECT FLDA FROM TBLA
WHERE FLDA < ALL (SELECT FLDB FROM TBLB);

— EXISTENCE SUBQUERIES —

```
SELECT FLDA FROM TBLA
WHERE EXISTS
(SELECT * FROM TBLB WHERE
TBLA.FLDA = TBLB.FLDB);

SELECT FLDA FROM TBLA
WHERE NOT EXISTS
(SELECT * FROM TBLB WHERE
TBLA.FLDA >= TBLB.FLDB);

SELECT FLDA, FLDB, FLDC FROM TBLA
WHERE EXISTS
(SELECT * FROM TBLB WHERE
TBLA.FLDA >= TBLB.FLDB
AND TBLA.FLDB = TBLB.FLDC);
```

— CORRELATED SUBQUERIES —

```
SELECT FLDA, FLDB FROM TBLA X
WHERE FLDA <=
(SELECT AVG(FLDA) FROM TBLA
WHERE FLDB = X.FLDB);
```

— UNION —

```
SELECT * FROM TBLA
UNION
SELECT * FROM TBLB;

SELECT * FROM TBLA
UNION
(SELECT * FROM TBLB
UNION
SELECT * FROM TBLC);

SELECT FLDA, FLDB FROM TBLA, TBLB
WHERE FLDA = FLDB
UNION
SELECT FLDC, FLDD FROM TBLC, TBLD
WHERE FLDC = FLDD
```

— CHANGING RECORDS —

UPDATE TBLA SET FLDA = 10;

UPDATE TBLA SET FLDA = 'Amber';

UPDATE TBLA SET
FLDA = 2, FLDB = 'Blue', FLDC = 59;

UPDATE TBLA SET FLDA = (FLDA + FLDB);

UPDATE TBLA SET FLDA = NULL;

UPDATE TBLA SET FLDA = NULL
WHERE FLDA >= 25;

UPDATE TBLA SET FLDA = 10
WHERE FLDB > 100 OR FLDC < 250;

UPDATE TBLA SET
FLDA = 5, FLDB = 'Green', FLDC = 36
WHERE FLDB = 'Yellow';

— CREATING RECORDS —

INSERT INTO TBLA VALUES (10, 30, 'Yellow');

INSERT INTO TBLA (FLDA, FLDB, FLDC)
VALUES (35, 127, 'Green');

INSERT INTO TBLA
SELECT * FROM TBLB;

INSERT INTO TBLA (FLDA, FLDB, FLDC)
SELECT FLDD, FLDE, FLDF FROM TBLB;

INSERT INTO TBLA (FLDA, FLDB, FLDC)
SELECT FLDD, FLDE, FLDF FROM TBLB
WHERE FLDE >= 125;

— DELETING RECORDS —

DELETE FROM TBLA;

DELETE FROM TBLA WHERE FLDA = 10;

DELETE FROM TBLA WHERE
((FLDA >= 25) AND (FLDB IS NOT NULL));

— CREATING VIEWS —

CREATE VIEW VWA AS SELECT * FROM TBLA;

CREATE VIEW VWA AS
SELECT FLDA, FLDE FROM TBLA;

CREATE VIEW VWA (FLDA, FLDB, FLDC) AS
SELECT FLDE, FLDF, FLDG FROM TBLA;

CREATE VIEW VWA AS
SELECT FLDA, FLDE FROM TBLA
WHERE FLDA >= 125;

CREATE VIEW VWA (FLDA, FLDB, FLDC) AS
SELECT TBLA.FLDE, TBLA.FLDF, TBLB.FLDG
FROM TBLA, TBLB;

— DELETING VIEWS —

DROP VIEW VWA;

— CREATING TABLES —

CREATE TABLE TBLA (FLDA NUMBER);

CREATE TABLE TBLA (FLDA CHAR(10));

CREATE TABLE TBLA
(FLDA NUMBER, FLDB CHAR(2));

CREATE TABLE TBLA
(FLDA NUMBER, FLDB CHAR(2),
FLDC CHAR(40), FLDD NUMBER));

— DELETING TABLES —

DROP TABLE TBLA;

Index